School Bus Drivers Who Care

20 Tips to Improve Student-Driver Relationships

By
Kelly E. Middleton

Edited by
Mike Mavilia Rochester

School Bus Drivers Who Care: 20 Tips to Improve Student-Driver Relationships

Published by Kelly E. Middleton
30 W. 8th St.
Newport, KY 41071
www.kellymiddleton.com

Edited by Mike Mavilia Rochester
Proofreader Michael Fedison
Layout by Sophie Hanks
Cover Design by Arash Jahani

ISBN (paperback): 978-1-7374608-4-8
ISBN (ebook): 978-1-7374608-5-5
Library of Congress Control Number: 2025923479

This book is dedicated to the extraordinary school bus drivers and monitors who play a vital role in our educational mission. Thank you for your unwavering commitment to safely transporting and caring for our students. Your dedication is the heartbeat of our educational system, and I am forever grateful for the spirit and warmth you bring to the journey every day.

Table of Contents

PREFACE 7

INTRODUCTION 11

1. The Best Bus Drivers Go Above and Beyond 21

2. The Best Bus Drivers Smile at Their Students 29

3. The Best Bus Drivers Make the Ride Enjoyable 35

4. The Best Bus Drivers Say Hello and Goodbye 45

5. The Best Bus Drivers Joke and
    Banter with Students 51

6. The Best Bus Drivers Have an Extra
    Pair of Eyes for Their Students 59

7. The Best Bus Drivers Know and
    Use Students' Names 67

8. The Best Bus Drivers Let the
    Students Know a Little About Themselves 73

v

9. The Best Bus Drivers Do Not Show Favoritism 79

10. The Best Bus Drivers Recover
    Well When Mistakes Are Made....................................85

11. The Best Bus Drivers Are in Control of Their Bus...95

12. The Best Bus Drivers Tell Students Why 101

13. The Best Bus Drivers Have a Clean School Bus........ 111

14. The Best Bus Drivers Walk in
    the Shoes of Their Students.................................119

15. The Best Bus Drivers Take Up for Students...........127

16. The Best Bus Drivers Know
    Students Are Always Watching Them......................133

17. The Best Bus Drivers Don't Do Dumb Things...........139

18. The Best Bus Drivers Enjoy Their Jobs...................145

19. The Best Bus Drivers Keep
    Backstage Issues Backstage.................................153

20. The Best Bus Drivers Are Professionals...................161

Supplemental Material 171

Other Books by Kelly E. Middleton 175

Works Cited...177

PREFACE

My First Job in Public Education

When I graduated from college with my teaching certificate, I was unsure what role I wanted to take on in education. As a former student-athlete, I naturally gravitated toward coaching students. In those days, coaching roles were often paired with teaching responsibilities. My search led me to an opportunity to coach under a mentor I admired. That meant I had to take on a teaching role as well. It turns out that the only available teaching position included the duty of driving a school bus.

At twenty-one, brimming with youthful confidence, I assured the interview panel that I could handle driving a bus, casually confirming it had an automatic transmission. Little did I know, my teaching assignment would involve reforming twelve students—each selected for significant behavioral challenges. Not only that, but I was to teach in a makeshift classroom: a trailer two miles from the nearest school, with no other staff around and no breaks. The job's complexity far exceeded anything I had anticipated—a harsh introduction to real-world responsibilities that stretched well beyond my college preparation.

I initially thought the biggest challenge would be managing the students. But it turned out, the real challenge was driving the bus.

On my first day, reality hit hard at the bus garage when I discovered that only manual transmission buses were available—a detail I certainly wish I'd known in advance. With no prior experience driving a stick shift, the task ahead felt overwhelming. I can only chuckle now at the memory of the bus garage staff likely stifling their laughter as I lurched and jerked my way through the lot.

In 1987, training requirements for bus drivers were surprisingly lax—something that seems almost inconceivable today. Thankfully, the rural community's children, many of whom were already familiar with operating tractors and other heavy equipment, became my unlikely instructors. In a confession made easier by the passage of time (and retirement), I'll admit: those students were instrumental in helping me get that bus rolling. During our earliest trips, they would shift gears for me while I pressed the clutch. Once I started getting the hang of it, they'd call out from their seats, "Time to shift, Mr. Middleton!"

It was a humbling introduction to education—and working life. Never in my wildest dreams did I imagine my first year would look like this.

That experience forged a deep respect for bus drivers that I carry to this day. I still remember those freezing winter mornings spent defrosting the windshield in total darkness and navigating slick roads with limited visibility. The responsibility and vigilance required behind the wheel left a lasting mark.

Despite the challenges—including the unfortunate replacement of two transmissions—the lessons of that first year have proven invaluable. They shaped the foundation of my thirty-two-year career in public education and instilled a lasting appreciation for the unsung heroes who safely transport our students each day. To those dedicated drivers, I offer my sincere gratitude for your unwavering commitment to our schools and the children we serve.

Why We Need a Customer Service Book for Public School Transportation

In *The School Bus Driver from the Black Lagoon* by Mike Thaler, a young student nervously anticipates his first school bus ride of the year—made even more intimidating by the fact that there's a new driver.[1] His anxiety grows as friends share wild and exaggerated stories: one claims the new driver is cruel; another insists he lets his guard dog do most of the driving. "He makes you pay for gas out of your lunch money," one of them says. The book is filled with humorous illustrations that bring these outrageous rumors to life.

In the end, all of the boy's fears disappear the moment the bus doors open and the driver welcomes him with a smile, even inviting him to sit up front.

This story reminds us how powerful a first impression can be, and how impactful a school bus driver is in shaping a student's day. I hope that bus drivers recognize the significant role they play in the lives of students. By taking the time to get to know their riders, they can not only create a more positive experience for students, but also find greater satisfaction and joy in their own work.

I've witnessed firsthand how important bus drivers are to our students. Over the years, I've ridden along on countless bus routes, observing how drivers' behaviors and interactions with students affected both the students and the atmosphere on the bus. Many of the stories in this book are rooted in these experiences.

Having written several books on customer service in public education, I've never written one specifically for school bus drivers. Yet they are among the most important frontline employees in our schools. Bus drivers are not only the first and last points of contact for our students each day—they also represent the values and culture of our school systems. A series of books on customer service in public schools would be incomplete without recognizing the essential contributions of the transportation department.

INTRODUCTION

Why do we need a book about customer service for bus drivers? Isn't it enough that you safely transport dozens of students to and from school every day? While that is, without question, the absolute top priority of any bus driver, it's not where the job begins or ends. In today's competitive education landscape, schools are asking every employee to bring their A-game. There are three reasons I believe bus drivers should offer the highest level of customer service to their student passengers.

The first—and most important reason—is the student experience. We want our students to feel as joyful and excited as the riders on Disney World shuttles, San Francisco cable cars, or open-top city tourism buses. While those drivers may be working for tips, a school bus driver's "tip" is the smile on a young rider's face.

The second reason? Job security. A bus full of happy students who go home raving about their driver to parents and teachers is a powerful asset. That kind of word-of-mouth endorsement makes you indispensable to your school or district. It's the holy grail of job security.

The third reason for this book is practical: great customer service makes your job easier—and safer. When students feel respected and valued, they tend to behave better. You'll deal with fewer discipline issues and enjoy more positive interactions—laughs, smiles, high fives, or even the occasional "You're my favorite driver!" Everyone wins when bus drivers bring their best. After all, don't we all want to be the person in our job or industry that people love, respect, and recommend? That's the power of great customer service.

Know the Competition and Know Why Customer Service Is Important

A friend once had a drive-thru experience that permanently soured him on a popular fast-food chain. When he asked for extra ketchup with his fries, he received one lonely packet. That small frustration was enough for him to swear off the chain for good. In business, customers often form their opinion of an entire company based on a single moment with a single employee. That one interaction can make or break loyalty.

Research shows just how hard it is to change a first impression. Think of a date or a job interview—you show up looking and acting your best. The same principle applies to bus drivers. That first day of school, when a student steps onto your bus, you're setting the tone for the entire year.

And it's not just the first impression that matters. The ride home is just as critical. Think about Disney's grand fireworks finale over the castle—it's their way of ending a guest's day on a high note. The bus ride home serves a similar purpose: it's the final act of a student's school day. Like a delicious dessert at the end of a meal, it's what they remember. And it can determine whether the day ends with a smile or a sigh.

"A corporation may spread itself over an entire world, may employ a thousand men, but the average person will form his judgement of it through contact with one individual. If that individual is rude or inefficient, it will take a lot of kindness and effectiveness to overcome that one bad impression."[2]

A failed first impression and a sour last contact can sink any business interaction—and the same is true in public education. The bus ride to and from school carries enormous weight in shaping a student's perception of their day.

Understanding the importance of customer service—even in school transportation—is just the first step. Every successful organization, including public schools, must keep an eye on the competition. A sure way to fall behind is to ignore those trying to surpass you. Do you think Pepsi ignores what Coke is doing? Or that cable TV isn't watching Netflix? Competition is real, and public education is no exception.

In my first book, *Who Cares*, I explore how Montgomery Ward failed to adapt. They were ahead of the game but ignored emerging competitors like Sears, who were building brick-and-mortar stores to challenge Montgomery Ward's catalog-only model. Eventually, Sears would lose much of their business to

Kmart and their blue light specials, and both later would close due to Walmart's expansion. Now, Walmart faces pressure from Amazon. The same pattern occurred in the auto industry. General Motors, Ford, and Chrysler paid little attention to Toyota—and now Toyota outsells all of them in the U.S.[3]

Public Education Is Quietly in Crisis

The public school system many of us took for granted is slowly being eroded by growing competition. While private schools have long drawn away some students, recent decades have seen explosive growth in alternatives—particularly charter schools and homeschooling. These options are pulling not just numbers, but often some of the most engaged and highest-performing students out of public education.

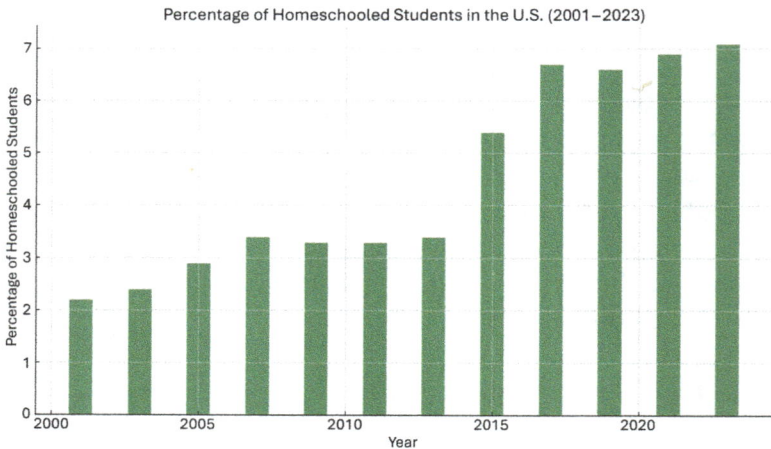

Percentage of Homeschooled Students in the U.S. (2001–2023)

So what does this mean for you? Lower enrollment in schools means fewer jobs. Public schools across the country have downsized and even closed because students moved to other, more attractive schooling options. If you haven't seen this happen at your school, it could be just around the corner. This is where customer service comes in.

Percentage of Students in the U.S. Enrolled in Charter Schools (2001–2023)

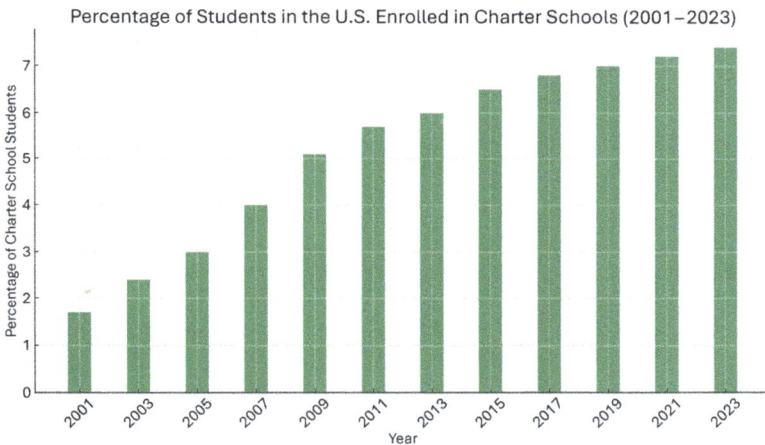

For bus drivers, viewing students as customers is especially relevant. You're the first point of contact each morning and the last person students see before heading home. That gives you a powerful opportunity to shape the tone of a student's entire day. In today's competitive educational landscape, the service you provide can significantly influence how families perceive the overall quality and appeal of the public school system.

Should public school employees be alarmed by the charts above? Why or why not?

A bus ride is more than a mode of transportation—it's an extension of the school environment. A ride that feels safe, friendly, and welcoming can set a student up for success. When bus drivers are warm, attentive, and genuinely invested in their passengers' well-being, the bus becomes more than a vehicle— it becomes a space of care and connection. According to my research, the single most important factor in a school employee's behavior is whether students believe that person truly cares about them. When students feel cared for, they're more trusting, show fewer behavioral issues, and even perform better academically.

"You can know the name of a bird in all the languages of the world, but when you're finished, you'll know absolutely nothing whatever about the bird. . . . So let's look at the bird and see what it's doing—that's what counts. I learned very early the difference between knowing the name of something and knowing something."[4] —Richard Feynman

Caring deeply for students is the heartbeat of this book. Each chapter offers tips and best practices used by exceptional bus drivers to show students they matter. While no one person may master all of them, implementing even a few of these strategies can go a long way in showing students that they're not just passengers—they're valued individuals. Driving a school bus, then, becomes more than just a job. It becomes a meaningful way to positively shape young lives.

In short, embracing the idea of customer service is essential for today's school bus drivers. You're not just steering a bus; you're shaping experiences, influencing perceptions, and helping public education remain both competitive and compassionate. In a world of growing educational choices, the quality of every part of a student's day—including the bus ride—matters more than ever.

School Bus Drivers Who Care:

20 Tips to Improve Student-Driver Relationships

1

The Best Bus Drivers Go Above and Beyond

> I think heroism is when somebody really goes above and beyond the call of duty and does something outstanding for either themselves or somebody else.[5]
> —John Assaraf, author

When I speak to audiences, I often ask them to turn to a neighbor and share a recent positive customer service experience. Almost immediately, the room fills with energy as people begin swapping stories. The most common theme? Someone went just a little above and beyond. It's like ordering a dozen doughnuts and watching the baker smile as they slip an extra one into the bag, saying, "This one's on me." That small gesture—unexpected and thoughtful—sticks with people. It turns a routine transaction into a memorable moment.

In the research I used in my book *Competing for Kids*, a study by J. D. Power uncovered something remarkable.[6] A little extra effort beats both low prices and high quality when it comes to winning over customers. Think about that. People don't just want a good deal; they want to feel seen, valued, and appreciated.

It's not about grand gestures. It's about that extra inch that says, "You matter."

Kenny Kelley: The Bus Driver with a Grandfather's Heart

For nine years, Kenny Kelley has been more than just a bus driver in Daviess County, Kentucky. He's been a figure of warmth, care, and consistency to the preschoolers who ride his bus each morning, earning him the affectionate nickname "the grandfather for every student."[7] At seventy-two years old, Kelley begins his day by brewing coffee for the bus dispatchers at 5:00 a.m., before preparing his bus to transport twenty preschoolers to Highland Elementary School.

Kelley's day doesn't end when the kids hop off the bus. Instead, he leads them into the school in a "choo-choo train," helps them through the breakfast line, and stays until every student—whether they arrived by bus or car—has received a hug and a word of encouragement. His caring attitude has made him a beloved figure among the students and staff alike.

Owens Saylor, the Daviess County superintendent, described Kelley's actions as the embodiment of a "servant's heart," a guiding principle of the school district. In recognition of his service, Kelley received the 2016 Fred Award from the Kentucky Association of School Administrators. The award, named after Fred Shea, a postal carrier who inspired the book *The Fred Factor* by Mark Sanborn, honors non-administrative school staff, students, or volunteers who go above and beyond to create a positive learning environment.[8] Though Kelley doesn't seek the limelight, his actions speak louder than words. "I just love being around kids," he says. "I've never had a day in nine years where I didn't want to go to work."

Kelley's journey to becoming a bus driver began after his retirement from delivering milk and snack cakes. After some encouragement from his wife, he applied to drive a bus. It was a decision that gave his life a renewed purpose. "It's just like I died and went to heaven," Kelley says of his job. Since then, he's formed deep connections with his students, even attending their games and recitals in his free time.

One student, Joseph Clements, who has Down syndrome, became an important part of Kelley's life after he spotted Kelley during bus transfers when Joseph was about six years old. For eight years and counting, Joseph has spent nearly every weekend at Kelley's house, and Kelley even considers him family: "He's not just family; he's like my arm or my leg," Kelley says.

Kelley's commitment to his students is unwavering—he has missed only four days of work in nine years. Now on his dream route, driving preschoolers, he hopes to continue making a difference for years to come. "If the good Lord lets me, at eighty years old I'll still be driving a school bus," Kelley says with a smile.

Mahlon Thomas: A Living Legend of Carlisle County

Mahlon Thomas isn't just a school bus driver in Carlisle County, Kentucky—he's a cherished community figure known for his kindness and generosity.[9] After nearly forty-one years of driving a bus, Thomas has left a lasting impact on his community through small but meaningful acts of kindness, such as creating scrapbooks for high school athletes, crafting memorial plaques for grieving families, and baking treats for his coworkers.

In recognition of his efforts, Thomas was awarded the 2023 Fred Award by the Kentucky Association of School Administrators.

Dustin Roberts, Carlisle County's director of pupil personnel and transportation, who nominated Thomas, said, "Mahlon's bond with both students and adults is obvious by the time he invests outside of the work environment. He is truly a living legend in Carlisle County."

Thomas grew up attending Carlisle County schools, later returning as a teacher before becoming a bus driver in the early 1980s. Over the years, he's built a reputation as someone students and adults can rely on. "I just try to be a friend," Thomas explains. "Someone they can talk to or depend on."

Though he's been thanked countless times for his acts of kindness, Thomas insists he doesn't do it for recognition. "You should love your fellow man and do whatever you can to make that individual happy or feel better about themselves," he says humbly.

After four decades of service, Thomas continues to bring joy and kindness to those around him, making the world a better place one small act at a time.

Going Above and Beyond: The Power of Small Acts of Care

Picture this: My child is in the eighth grade, playing on the middle school basketball team. Tonight, the team has a game about seventy miles away, with two other matches lined up beforehand—a sixth-grade game and a seventh-grade game. Since I'm unfamiliar with the town and the gym, I decide to follow the team bus in my car.

Before the bus departs, the driver distributes a piece of paper with the exact address of the gym to all the parents who are driving to the game. But it's more than just directions. The paper also includes recommendations for good places to eat and shop in the area, along with personal tips from the driver. Later that evening, as the game is in full swing, I glance up into the stands and spot the bus driver cheering enthusiastically for my child and the rest of the team. At one point, she even voices her disapproval when the referee makes a questionable call against our team—her loyalty and passion are clear.

As a parent, I felt deeply moved. This driver wasn't just transporting our kids; she genuinely cared about their success and well-being. It was a comforting thought—knowing that my child was part of a team where even the bus driver had their back. In that moment, I realized just how fortunate we were to be part of a community where people go above and beyond their roles.

Another vivid memory comes to mind, from my own childhood. I had to change schools and was placed in a large, unfamiliar school district. Halfway home on my first day, I realized I had boarded the wrong bus. It was already a tough day, and now

I found myself headed to who knows where, surrounded by strangers. As the bus gradually emptied, I started tearing up, feeling lost and alone. Soon, it was just the driver and me.

Noticing my distress, the driver reassured me. He promised to get me home safely and made sure I knew that everything was going to be okay. True to his word, he took me to my house and later that evening even called my parents. He wanted to confirm which bus I should take the next day and checked in to see how I was doing, knowing I'd had a rough day.

In both instances, these bus drivers were superheroes to my family and me. Their small acts of kindness and reassurance left a lasting impact. As a student, I would never dream of misbehaving on their buses—not just out of fear of consequences, but out of respect for their care and dedication. And if I ever did, I know my parents would stand firmly by these drivers, trusting their judgment.

So now, I challenge you. Reflect on the best customer service experiences you've ever had. Chances are, they involved someone going above and beyond the basic requirements of their job. What might happen if we all applied that same principle in our work, our relationships, and our communities? The smallest gestures can leave the biggest impact.

Reflection/Discussion Questions

- After reading the stories about bus drivers who received a Fred Award, how many practices can you find that are named in this book?

- Can you give an example of when you have received above-and-beyond customer service? How did it make you feel?

- In the stories above, what do you believe motivates these drivers to give this type of customer service each day?

- What are some examples of how you give above and beyond customer service? What are some possible other ideas you might like to try?

2

The Best Bus Drivers Smile at Their Students

66

Peace begins with a smile.[10]
—Mother Teresa

99

One consistent piece of feedback I've encountered regarding my customer service books is their simplicity and reliance on what many consider to be "common sense." Reflecting on my journey as an author, I was initially taken aback by the need to dedicate an entire chapter to the power of a smile in the context of viewing students as customers. However, the insights gleaned from interviewing hundreds of students, coupled with an extensive review of thousands of pieces of research, cemented my conviction. The evidence is irrefutable: students respond positively to respect and are more inclined to excel when adults greet them with a smile.

My revelation shouldn't have been unexpected. Reflecting on the principles of the 7-38-55 rule formulated by psychology professor Albert Mehrabian, it's clear that face-to-face communication is overwhelmingly influenced by nonverbal cues.[11] A staggering 55 percent of our message is transmitted through body language, with mere words contributing only 7 percent and tone of voice completing the remaining 38 percent.

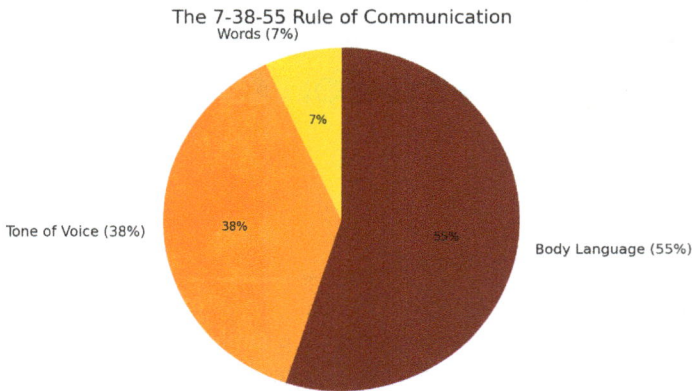

The 7-38-55 Rule of Communication
Words (7%)

7%

Tone of Voice (38%)   38%   55%   Body Language (55%)

The Power of a Smile

Imagine this scenario. Every morning, at precisely 7:00 a.m., the rumble of bus seventeen echoed through the sleepy streets of Willowbrook. Mrs. Ellis, the bus driver, was known for her punctuality. But more than that, she was known for her smile.

For over ten years, Mrs. Ellis had driven the same route. Her salt-and-pepper hair curled and fell gently on her shoulders and her thick-rimmed glasses perched on her nose as she greeted each student with a gentle grin. It wasn't much—a quick upturn of the lips—but it was enough to brighten the gloomy morning routine for many of the kids. They all had different lives and different stories, but there was something they all shared: they knew Mrs. Ellis would be there each day, smiling.

One cold, gray November morning, as the bus pulled up to stop number twenty-three, Mrs. Ellis noticed something different. Abby, one of the quietest students, a high school freshman who always sat in the middle of the bus, got on board with her head down. She didn't look up when Mrs. Ellis said, "Good morning, Abby." She responded with only a small nod, and Mrs. Ellis noticed her eyes were swollen with dark circles beneath them.

That whole week, Abby's demeanor stayed the same. She trudged onto the bus, and though Mrs. Ellis tried to greet her warmly each morning, she seemed lost in a fog of sadness. The bus driver made sure to smile a little wider each time Abby boarded, hoping that somehow it would help.

By Friday, Mrs. Ellis was beginning to doubt if her daily smile could make any difference. That morning, when Abby stepped onto the bus, she hesitated for the first time. Instead of immediately walking to her seat, she stood by the front for a moment, looking at Mrs. Ellis.

"Thank you," she whispered, her voice barely audible above the hum of the engine. Mrs. Ellis looked at her, surprised. "For always smiling," Abby continued, her eyes tearing up. "This week's been . . . hard. I just wanted to say, it helped knowing someone would be happy to see me, even if it's just for a moment."

Mrs. Ellis felt a warmth rise in her chest. She had no idea what was going on in Abby's life, but in that moment, she realized the importance of the small, seemingly insignificant gestures she made every day. A smile—her smile—had made a difference.

And not just for Abby. As the weeks went on, Mrs. Ellis noticed the ripple effect of her kindness. Abby's smile returned, little by little, and as the days passed, she even began greeting her bus driver with a small wave and a quiet "Good morning." Other students, seeing the small interactions between Mrs. Ellis and Abby, began to smile a little more, too.

By the end of the school year, Mrs. Ellis realized that the simple act of smiling wasn't just a routine—it was a lifeline. A lifeline for Abby, for the other students, and, in a way, for herself. Her job wasn't just to drive the bus; it was to be a steady, positive presence in the lives of these kids, some of whom might not experience kindness elsewhere.

As the final bell of the school year rang and the students boarded the bus for the last time, Mrs. Ellis gave each one her usual smile. But this time, when Abby stepped onto the bus, she didn't just return the smile—she handed her a small, folded note.

"Thank you for seeing me," it read. "You made all the difference."

Mrs. Ellis tucked the note into her jacket pocket, her smile widening.

This concept was brought home to me during my tenure as an assistant superintendent when a beloved teacher tragically passed away. The outpouring of grief and respect from students was overwhelming, culminating in a Facebook memorial with over a thousand posts. Remarkably, many students who had never been taught by him shared their memories. The most frequent tribute paid to this teacher was not about his lessons, but the simple fact that he always offered them a smile. These heartfelt messages from students matched with Professor Mehrabian's findings on communication and underscored a profound truth: the act of smiling, seemingly trivial to us adults, can leave an indelible impact on our students.

Reflection/Discussion Questions

- What does good body language look like? What about bad body language?

- Do you know some people who just look like they are always in a bad mood? What are they doing incorrectly? In your opinion, has anyone ever had a conversation with them about their body language?

- Do you know some people who look like they are always in a good mood? What are some of their facial characteristics?

- Talk with a partner about good and bad examples of nonverbal communication.

- Find a partner or a mirror and practice smiling. Give feedback to each other. What are you doing well? What can be improved?

3

The Best Bus Drivers Make the Ride Enjoyable

> " Life is about the journey, not the destination. So roll down the windows, turn up the music, and enjoy the ride. "
> —Unknown

Have you ever ridden cable cars or street cars in San Francisco? What about a fun train ride to a theme park or from the park back to your car? Did the driver try to make it a fun, pleasurable trip? The best tour guides and businesses know that the fun is not necessarily about the destination, but the journey.

Take Disney, for example. Disney World and Disneyland operate a network of shuttle buses to bring passengers to and from their parks. One thing the Disney corporation does consistently is inject every little detail of the customer's experience with fun. On my family's first trip to Disney World, we pulled into the parking lot excited to jump on the rides. But that quickly faded when we realized our spot was far from the entrance—a sea of cars stretched before us, and the distant silhouette of Cinderella's Castle felt miles away. I let out a sigh, but as soon as I closed the car door, I heard the cheerful clang of a bell.

A shuttle train pulled up, and the driver—a man with a big grin and a pair of Mickey Mouse ears—waved us over. "Hop on in, folks! The magic express is ready to roll!" he announced, his voice as lively as the music spilling from the park in the distance.

"Looks like you parked in the wilderness," he said with a laugh as we climbed aboard. "Good thing I'm here to bring you back to civilization—and the fun!" His enthusiasm was contagious. We all laughed, and suddenly, the long trek from our parking spot didn't seem so bad.

As the shuttle rolled forward, the driver shared his favorite tips and secrets about the park. "Now, if you're looking for the best spot to watch the fireworks, there's this little area near the bridge by the castle—perfect view and not too crowded." He winked as if sharing a well-kept secret. "And don't miss the pineapple Dole Whip. It's practically a requirement."

He told us stories of his favorite rides and how he'd sneak onto Space Mountain before the crowds hit. "Nothing like flying through the stars when you've still got your morning coffee buzz," he joked. And he shared how the Pirates of the Caribbean ride still gave him a thrill, even after a decade of working at the park.

What Makes a Great School Bus Driver?

If I asked a transportation director, a superintendent, a principal, and a student to list the qualities of a great bus driver, I believe I would get a huge variety of answers. Here are just a few possible answers.

1. **Safety-Oriented:** The primary role of a school bus driver is to transport students safely. They should be knowledgeable about and adhere to all traffic laws, safety protocols, and emergency procedures. Very few to zero accidents.

2. **Reliability and Punctuality:** Drivers who do not miss work, arriving on time to ensure that students are picked up and dropped off as scheduled.

3. **Patience and Calm Demeanor:** Working with children, especially in a confined space like a bus, requires patience. Drivers may need to manage noisy or energetic behavior calmly and effectively.

4. **Good Communication Skills:** Effective communication with students, parents, school administrators, and other drivers is crucial. They should be able to convey information clearly and listen to concerns or instructions.

5. **Physical and Mental Fitness:** Driving a bus requires physical health and mental alertness. Drivers should be able to handle the physical demands of the job and remain focused and alert while driving.

6. **Problem-Solving Skills:** Drivers may encounter unexpected situations such as traffic delays, road closures, or student conflicts. The ability to quickly and effectively resolve these issues is important.

7. **Discipline and Classroom Management:** Maintaining discipline on the bus is important for safety. Drivers should establish and enforce rules in a fair and respectful manner.

8. **Training and Certification:** Drivers must have the appropriate driving licenses, certifications, and training, including knowledge of first aid and emergency response.

9. **Attention to Detail:** Paying attention to details like bus maintenance, student attendance, and route planning is essential for a smooth operation.

10. **Resilience and Adaptability:** Flexibility in dealing with changes in weather, routes, or schedules, and the ability to remain composed under stress, are important traits.

11. **Professionalism:** This includes dressing appropriately, being respectful to everyone, and maintaining confidentiality where necessary.

12. **Numerous "International Bus Roadeo Awards":** Demonstrating the driver's skills on the big yellow bus.

Every turn, every joke, every fun fact made the shuttle ride a little adventure of its own. By the time we reached the park entrance, my family and I were laughing so hard our sides hurt. We waved goodbye to our driver as we stepped off the shuttle. "Hope I see y'all later tonight when you're heading back! Remember, I'm your chariot driver!" he called out, tipping his Mickey ears.

As we walked through the gates, the magic of Disney World began to wrap around us. But I couldn't help but think that the first ride of the day—the one with that friendly shuttle driver— might just be the best one. And as the sun began to dip behind the castle that night, I found myself hoping we'd see him again, to end our day the way it started—with a little extra magic.

Not only did this employee get his customers to the park safely and in a timely manner, but he also injected some excitement into the passengers' wait to get to the fun part. This is the backbone of making any bus ride enjoyable. It's your chance to channel your inner actor, do goofy voices, sing off-key at the top of your lungs, or even show your oddball side. Your bus ride is a chance to make a unique and entertaining experience for your student passengers.

The Yellow Limousine

A bus driver in a large school district in Colorado acknowledges every student who boards the bus. Randomly, as a student boards, she'll ask the student for his or her bus pass (her district doesn't use passes) just to get a reaction. When the kids respond that they do not have one, she says, "Well, you will just have to take a seat and have fun."

When the bus is almost full, she tells the kids to sing "Happy Birthday" to the next kid who gets on the bus. The reaction is always priceless. Sometimes she will ask the students with really cool shoes what size they are, and would they mind trading for the day?

The driver says the students enjoy this type of humor. She is also letting them know that she notices them and cares about them. She has had to discipline students much less often and they are having a lot more fun on their seventy-seven-passenger yellow limousine.

The Magic Ride

Mrs. Jeffers wasn't your ordinary school bus driver. From the moment she got behind the wheel of bus number forty-seven, she had a mission: to make every ride more than just a ride. She believed that the few minutes between home and school were a golden opportunity—one where she could turn the otherwise mundane trip into something the students looked forward to every day.

She had grown up in San Francisco, where cable car drivers were local legends. They didn't just operate machinery—they made people feel like they were part of something special, like they were on an adventure. Mrs. Jeffers brought that same spirit to her school bus, determined to make the trip memorable, not just a daily grind.

On her first day, she glanced into the large rearview mirror and saw rows of blank faces, some tired, others bored, headphones in, lost in their own worlds. That wouldn't do, she thought. She wanted the students to feel excited, even if just for those fifteen minutes.

"Good morning, everybody!" she called out with enthusiasm that felt out of place for a school bus, but she didn't care. "Today, you're on the most magical bus in the world. As we start our journey, look to your right—those clouds? They're floating cotton candy! And on the left, those trees are secretly ancient guardians protecting the road. Buckle up—this is going to be a wild ride!"

The kids looked up, confused. A few rolled their eyes, but some smiled, intrigued. Over the next few weeks, her greetings became more elaborate, more theatrical. She began narrating the ride like a tour guide.

"And up ahead, folks, we're passing by the famous 'mystery stoplight,' which sometimes turns red . . . but today, it's green because it knows we're on a mission!" Mrs. Jeffers grinned as the bus rolled through the intersection, and a few giggles trickled through the seats.

The students started to talk about the stories she told, comparing notes. Some kids even started calling out to Mrs. Jeffers when they got on board.

"What's the adventure today, Mrs. Jeffers?"

"Oh, you'll see!" she'd reply with a wink. "Hold on tight, there might be dragons on the freeway today!"

Over time, the ride transformed. No longer was it just the daily shuffle to school—it became something the students anticipated. They began to leave their phones in their backpacks, listening to the stories, laughing at the jokes, and sometimes adding their own. Mrs. Jeffers created a world where the school bus wasn't just a vehicle but an experience.

But it wasn't just the stories. On Fridays, she played upbeat music over the speakers, inviting the students to start their weekend early. "DJ Jeffers on the mix today!" she'd announce, and the students would clap and sing along to the latest pop hits, turning the morning ride into a small celebration.

One particularly hard winter, when the snowbanks made everything seem bleak, Mrs. Jeffers decorated the inside of the bus with twinkling lights and paper snowflakes the kids had made. She told them they were traveling through a winter wonderland where snow angels ruled the land, and suddenly, the gray days felt a little brighter.

By the end of the school year, the students had changed. They no longer dragged themselves onto the bus; they leaped on with anticipation, eager to see what Mrs. Jeffers had in store for them. Some of the quieter kids who used to sit at the back now chatted with their classmates, their laughter filling the bus. For others, the stories and music became the best part of their day—something they carried with them through the stress of school.

One day, as Mrs. Jeffers pulled up to the final stop, a fifth grader named Rachel lingered a little longer before stepping off the bus. She looked up at the driver, shyly tugging at her backpack straps.

"Thanks for making the bus ride fun, Mrs. Jeffers," she said softly. "It's the best part of my day."

Mrs. Jeffers smiled, her heart swelling. There it was—the tip she worked for, the one that mattered more than anything else. She knew it then, in that simple thank you, that what she had been doing wasn't just a job. She was giving the kids something they would remember, something that could make their days just a little better.

And in return, they had given her something, too—proof that a simple ride could be transformed into something magical with just a little effort and a whole lot of heart.

Reflection/Discussion Questions

- Does it sound like fun to be a student on this bus? How about being the driver?

- What are some other ways to connect with students when they are loading and unloading the bus?

- Have you ever ridden a cable car, train, plane, etc. where the person driving or steering the vehicle tried to entertain the group? Discuss the situation. Did you enjoy the experience?

- Could a bus driver or bus aide be the most important person in a student's life?

4

The Best Bus Drivers Say Hello and Goodbye

> You know what happens when you say 'hello' or 'good morning?' You make a connection. And isn't that what being human is all about?[12]
> —Phillip Rosenthal, television writer/producer

The impact of employees who are the first and last point of contact with customers is immense. Such employees, I believe, embody the essence of the organization and merit being among the most valued and actively sought-after members of the team. They have a chance to make a great first impression on the customer while also having a chance to be their last good memory of the day. In the context of schools, bus drivers often hold this crucial role for students. Simple actions like a smile or a friendly greeting can significantly influence a student's experience. In one of my books, *Simply the Best*, we surveyed students of varying grade levels. I'll refer to these surveys throughout this book. Our findings showed that students feel more positively about and are more engaged with adults who acknowledge them daily.[13] Despite the simplicity of these actions, their frequent mention by students cannot be ignored. It suggests that fostering these positive interactions might be an area for growth in public education. Our research also found that students thrive under the care of adults they like and trust.

While it may seem like such a small, insignificant gesture to smile, say hello, say goodbye, or say have a nice weekend, our interviews with students tell us that this means so much to our primary customers, the students. When students are asked why certain adults are so loved in our public schools, we are routinely told over and over again, "They speak to us each day." I have to admit, as an author, some of these gestures seemed so simple that I felt they should not be included in a book. However, these simple responses were so numerous I could not leave them out. Based on the sheer number of responses, I now believe that lots of adults in public education do not smile and speak to students regularly. I also hate to say that in public education we really need to teach adults how to smile and start conversations with children. After all, our research tells us that students will behave better and learn more from adults they like.

The Bridge Between Days

Every morning, the yellow school bus rumbled down the streets of the thriving metropolis of Springfield. And every morning, Mr. Hawkins was there, seated behind the big steering wheel with a gentle smile. He was the first face the students saw before stepping into the whirlwind of their school day, and the last as they returned home, weary or excited.

Mr. Hawkins had been driving the same route for over fifteen years, ferrying students back and forth, watching them grow up in small, meaningful ways. He wasn't just a bus driver. To many students, he was a steady, kind presence—someone they could count on in the unpredictable worlds of middle school and high school.

"Good morning, Ellie! You've got that math test today, right? You'll do great," he said one Tuesday morning as Ellie shuffled onto the bus, biting her lip nervously. His words, simple as they were, landed softly, making her feel just a little less anxious.

At first, the students didn't think much of Mr. Hawkins's daily greetings or farewells. Some mornings, they would barely respond, too absorbed in their phones or their own thoughts. But over time, something about his consistency began to feel like more than just habit.

"Goodbye, Mateo! Keep that smile going," he'd call out every afternoon, and without fail, Mateo would look up, surprised at first, but eventually returning a small wave and grin as he stepped off the bus.

It wasn't long before the students began to look forward to those words, those brief exchanges. It was as if, in those moments, Mr. Hawkins reminded them that they were seen and that their presence mattered amidst the hustle and bustle of the city. Even when they were having bad days, Mr. Hawkins's steady "hello" and "goodbye" were like a lifeline, reminding them that someone cared enough to notice.

One winter morning, the bus rolled to a stop in front of Olivia's apartment. She hesitated, sitting on the stoop in the cold, wondering if it was even worth going to school that day. Her grades were slipping, and her parents were too busy to notice. But then she saw Mr. Hawkins wave, the warmth of his smile cutting through the chill.

"Morning, Olivia! We've got sunshine today. You ready to tackle it?"

His words weren't profound, but they struck a chord in her. Maybe, she thought, she *was* ready to tackle the day, just because someone expected her to. As she stepped onto the bus, she gave him a small nod. That day, she handed in the assignment she'd been avoiding for weeks.

Over the years, Mr. Hawkins never realized just how much his simple greetings meant. He never knew that his words had pulled students like Olivia out of dark places, had boosted Ellie's confidence before that test, or had given Mateo a reason to smile on days when he felt invisible.

To Mr. Hawkins, it was just part of the job. But to the students, it was much more. He was the bridge between the chaos of the school day and the comfort of home—a reminder, twice a day, that in a place where it was easy to be forgotten or unnoticed, someone cared enough to see them and offer a kind greeting and a familiar face.

And as the years passed, perhaps students who had long since left for college or started their first jobs would often think back, remembering the gentle voice of Mr. Hawkins, the school bus driver who made a difference just by being there and saying "hello" and "goodbye" every single day.

Reflection/Discussion Questions

- Have you ever felt like someone refused to acknowledge you? How did that make you feel?

- Have you ever been accused of not speaking to someone? How did that make you feel?

- Some of the best customer service companies have policies that state their employees are supposed to speak to guests who come within five feet of them. Would that be a good policy for school district transportation employees? Why or why not?

5

The Best Bus Drivers Joke and Banter with Students

> "Sir," she said, "you are no gentleman!"
> "An apt observation," he answered airily.
> "And, you, Miss, are no lady."[14]
> —Margaret Mitchell, *Gone with the Wind*

Students often enjoy a lighthearted debate or teasing with bus drivers, which can create a vibrant atmosphere on the bus. Engaging in friendly banter shows students that educators are approachable and can foster a sense of connection. For instance, teachers may playfully challenge a student's sports team preference or gently critique their movie recommendations, which can be a way to enter a student's world momentarily. Research indicates that lighthearted interactions between adults and students can significantly enhance relationships and create a positive environment.[15]

However, it's essential to avoid sarcasm, as it can be misunderstood and potentially hurtful. It's also crucial to maintain a professional boundary; adults should be role models, not friends, to preserve respect. Above all, before engaging in jest, students must feel that their bus drivers genuinely care about them. Personalized interactions, like using a special nickname, can be endearing, provided they are received positively and are respectful of individual preferences. Balancing humor with professionalism is key to a healthy student relationship.

Morning Chuckles with Mr. Thompson

Every morning, as students boarded bus forty-two, they were greeted by Mr. Thompson's cheerful voice: "Good morning! Ready for another day of adventure?" He had a knack for remembering each student's interests. To the soccer enthusiasts, he'd quip, "Score any goals in your dreams last night?" For the budding artists, he'd ask, "Paint any masterpieces in your sleep?" These personalized jokes made students feel seen and valued. Over time, even the shyest kids began sharing their stories, knowing Mr. Thompson would listen and respond with a witty remark. This daily banter transformed the bus ride from a mundane routine into a cherished part of their day.

The Riddle Master of Route Fifteen

Ms. Garcia, the driver of route fifteen, had a unique tradition. Every Friday, she presented a riddle to her passengers. "What has keys but can't open locks?" she'd ask, sparking a flurry of guesses. The following Monday, she'd reveal the answer ("A piano!") and reward the students who had guessed correctly with a small treat. This playful interaction not only made the rides enjoyable but also fostered a sense of community among the students. They began collaborating, discussing possible answers, and eagerly anticipating the next riddle. Ms. Garcia's lighthearted approach turned the bus into a space of camaraderie and fun.

A Few Riddles to Share with Students

There are countless ways to joke with students. Here are just a few. What topics could you joke with your students about?

1. "Why did the math book look sad? Because it had too many problems."
2. "Why don't scientists trust atoms? Because they make up everything."
3. "Why did the bicycle fall over? Because it was two-tired."
4. "Why can't you give Elsa a balloon? Because she will let it go."
5. "What do you call a dinosaur with an extensive vocabulary? A thesaurus."
6. "Why did the computer go to the doctor? Because it had a virus."
7. "Why was the math lecture so long? The teacher kept going off on a tangent."

8. "Why did the golfer bring two pairs of pants? In case she got a hole in one."

9. "Why did the music teacher need a ladder? To reach the high notes."

10. "What do you call a cow with no legs? Ground beef."

11. "What do you call a pig that knows karate? A pork chop."

12. "What do you call an alligator in a vest? An investigator."

13. "Why did the picture go to jail? Because it was framed."

14. "What do you call a snowman with a six-pack? An abdominal snowman."

15. "What do you call a dog magician? A labracadabrador."

16. "What do you call a boomerang that doesn't come back? A stick."

17. "What do you call a shoe made of a banana? A slipper."

18. "What do you call a rabbit with fleas? Bugs Bunny."

19. "What do you call a dinosaur that never gives up? A try-try-try-ceratops."

20. "What do you call a bee that can't make up its mind? A maybe."

Playful Bantering on the Bus

The Great Soda Debate

Mrs. Jenkins had a talent for finding the most outrageous arguments to spark giggles on her route. One morning, she announced to the bus: "All right, listen up. Coke is the undisputed king of soft drinks. Pepsi is just . . . sugar pretending to be soda!"

The students erupted in a chorus of disagreements. "No way, Mrs. Jenkins!" shouted James. "Pepsi has more flavor!"

"Flavor?" Mrs. Jenkins laughed. "You mean watered-down cola with a sprinkle of despair? Nah, Coke is the champion."

For weeks, this banter continued. James would bring Pepsi facts he'd found online, and Mrs. Jenkins would counter with her own "Coke superiority" arguments. Eventually, the entire bus joined the debate. Students even started bringing sodas to compare. By the end of the school year, they weren't just riders—they were a team united by laughter and fizz-fueled fun.

Fast Cars and Faster Comebacks

Mr. Carter, the self-proclaimed "Coolest Bus Driver in Town," loved bragging about his imaginary red Corvette. "That thing's so fast," he'd say, "it left a Tesla eating dust at a green light yesterday."

"You can't even outrun a minivan, Mr. Carter!" shouted Mia, a fifth grader with a sharp wit.

"Minivan? Mia, that Tesla was trying to keep up so hard, it ran out of battery before the stop sign!"

Mia, undeterred, grinned. "Well, my dad's Tesla could beat your Corvette any day, even if it was on eco-mode!"

From then on, Mr. Carter made a daily habit of finding Mia to "rev up" the rivalry. He'd mimic car noises as he pulled up to her stop, hollering, "Vroom-vroom! Ready to lose today?" And Mia would fire back, "Only if you don't chicken out this time!" Their pretend car rivalry became a highlight of the bus ride, drawing cheers and laughter from the other kids.

Fun Bantering Topics

1. "That's not your favorite color? No way—it's orange. I can tell by your face!"

2. "Cats are way cooler than dogs; don't even try to argue!"

3. "Pizza with pineapple is the best. If you disagree, you're just wrong."

4. "Your favorite superhero? Nah, mine could beat them with one hand tied behind their cape."

5. "I bet I could finish that math homework faster than you!"

6. "Oh, you're good at *Fortnite*? I'd still crush you in a TikTok dance-off!"

7. "Your favorite teacher isn't cooler than me. Nice try, though."

8. "*Minecraft*? I built a mansion in *Roblox*—beat that!"

9. "How's your team doing? Still losing, right?"

10. "Chocolate ice cream is the worst. There, I said it!"

11. "Football is way better than basketball. No contest."

12. "Your bus stop is the slowest one. I time it."

13. "Your favorite singer? Their last album put me to sleep."

14. "What's with your shoelaces? Did your dog tie them for you?"

15. "Oh, you like video games? I'd crush you in *Mario Kart*."

16. "Your joke was funny—if you're a grandpa!"

17. "You're going to have to teach me that dance move you were doing this morning—looks like you've got some serious moves!"

18. "You always get on the bus with the best attitude. What's your secret to starting the day with a smile?"

19. "I see you're reading that book again. Are you trying to finish it before we reach the school?"

20. "I noticed you brought your lunch today. Got any extra for the person who drives you around every day?"

Reflection/Discussion Questions

- Can you give some examples of a time when you joked with a student, and it strengthened the relationship?

- Did you ever have a bus driver, teacher, or other school employee joke and banter with you when you were a student? How did it make you feel?

- Did you ever try to banter with a student or another adult and it did not go so well? What went wrong? How could it have been improved?

- Did you have a favorite adult in your life who you enjoyed bantering back and forth with?

6

The Best Bus Drivers Have an Extra Pair of Eyes for Their Students

> " Sometimes, one needs another pair of eyes to see things clearly.[16]
> —Aguidon, author "

The school year can be a series of ups and downs for students. Many struggle with issues that schools don't even know about. That's where school employees can have a huge impact on a student. Watching out for any different behavior can lead to the school understanding what's going on in a student's life and deciding what to do about it. That's what having an extra pair of eyes for the students means and bus drivers have a unique opportunity to help their riders.

As the first person to see a child in the morning and the last to see a child at the end of the academic day, school bus drivers get to see mood shifts in their passengers. They may even pick up on a child who is upset. It could be that their beloved pet has died or there was a family issue like divorce or abuse. In order to help, bus drivers need to be keenly aware of what resources the school district has for its students. Family resource centers, youth service centers, peer mediation, and other programs are often available to families. The best bus drivers will talk with the student's parents or make a suggestion to the school guidance counselor or principal, or even talk to the student themselves. If your school has a process where drivers can report issues, perhaps the school can help the students and keep them from acting out in class or doing something that is not in their best interests.

In addition to resources for intervention, noticing that a student has an interest or talent in music or is very athletic, bus drivers can encourage students to reach out to the appropriate club or group. Referring students to co-curricular and extracurricular programs is another way to be the extra set of eyes watching out for the students' best interests.

While writing this book, I came across an article from Louisville, Kentucky, where a school bus driver noticed that one of his regular riders wasn't his usual upbeat self.[17]

Larry Farrish Jr., who drives for Jefferson County Public Schools, saw that a first grader named Levi was sitting quietly by the side of the road, coat pulled over his head, crying. That was a big change from the cheerful kid he usually picked up.

When Farrish asked what was going on, he found out the reason behind Levi's tears—it was Pajama Day at Engelhard Elementary, and Levi didn't have any pajamas to wear.

"That just wasn't like Levi," Farrish later said in a school district release. "It broke my heart. I just wanted him to have a good day—no kid should feel left out over something as simple as Pajama Day."

With seven years behind the wheel, Farrish sees his job as more than just driving. "Once those kids leave their parents, they become my responsibility," he said. "Yes, I get them to school safely, but I also try to bring some happiness into their lives."

So, after dropping off his students and finishing his morning route, Farrish headed to Family Dollar. He picked up a few sets of pajamas in various sizes, then circled back to the school to see if Levi could come to the front office.

When Levi came down the hallway and saw what was waiting for him, he lit up. "That smile—it turned the whole day around for both of us," Farrish said.

Levi quickly changed into some football-themed pajamas and went back to join his classmates. Later, a JCPS administrator shared the story on Facebook, and it blew up—more than three hundred people chimed in to thank and celebrate Mr. Larry for his kindness.

One parent, Maggie Willacker, commented, "Mr. Larry is the absolute best. We were lucky to have him as our bus driver for four years. Top notch human." Dozens of others echoed her feelings, happy to see a story like this making the rounds in their feeds—proof that a small act of kindness can make a big impact.

On the Lookout for Bullying

Being an extra set of eyes is another way school bus drivers can impact their students' lives. The school day is so hectic, school employees can be too busy doing their jobs to notice a student who is struggling emotionally. Often, it's the downtime—whether it's in the cafeteria, recess, or the bus rides—when a school employee can see certain dynamics playing out. Bullying is a great example, since it often takes place when students do not have a task at hand. As a bus driver, you have a window into these dynamics and can help diffuse or even prevent them.

Every morning, as the sun barely crested the horizon, Mr. Walters climbed into his bus. The leather seat, worn and molded to his shape over the years, felt like home. He loved this bus. It was old, and the paint was peeling in some places, but it was his. More importantly, it carried the kids—the kids he had watched grow up year after year, some shy and small at first, then taller and confident as they reached high school.

The students like to joke that he had an extra set of eyes. But there was truth in it. He could always tell when a new student stepped onto his bus, even before they climbed the first step. This morning, he spotted a small girl with a pink backpack standing at the curb. She was new—he could see it in the way her hands clenched the straps of her bag, and her eyes flicked nervously to the other kids.

"Hey there," he said, his voice warm and inviting. "First day, huh?"

She nodded, her eyes wide and uncertain.

"Well, you've got the best seat in the house right up here," he said, gesturing to the front row. She hesitated, then climbed in, relieved. He gave her a wink. "Don't worry, kiddo. We'll get you there safe."

As the bus rumbled along, Mr. Walters glanced in his mirror, his eyes not just on the road but on the students behind him. He could always tell when something was off. Today, it was Tom—a usually chatty fifth grader—staring out the window, and not saying a word.

When they pulled up to the school and the kids filed out, Mr. Walters saw Tom linger, dragging his feet.

"Hey, Tom," he called out, "hold on a second."

Tom looked up, his face a mix of confusion and relief. Mr. Walters got up from his seat and walked down the aisle. "Everything okay, bud?"

Tom shrugged, but his eyes were red, and his shoulders sagged. Mr. Walters knew that look; it was the look of a kid carrying too much weight for his small frame. He patted Tom on the shoulder. "Why don't we walk in together? Sometimes, all you need is a little company."

Tom nodded, and together they walked through the front doors of the school, side by side. Mr. Walters knew he couldn't solve everything, but he could be there. Sometimes, that was all a kid needed. When he left Tom at his first class, he gave Tom a smile and said, "Have a great day." Tom returned his smile and walked into the classroom, looking a little lighter than before.

On cold days, Mr. Walters's eyes seemed sharper than ever. He noticed the kids shivering, trying to hide it. Once, he'd spotted a boy wearing shoes with holes in them. That evening, he called a friend who worked at a local thrift shop, and the next morning, there was a new pair of shoes waiting on the boy's seat.

Mr. Walters never said a word about these small acts of kindness; he just gave a nod or a warm smile when the kids looked his way. His extra set of eyes saw more than just who was getting on and off the bus. They saw the worries, the fears, and the quiet struggles that the kids carried with them. And as long as he was behind the wheel, he'd do everything in his power to make sure those kids felt safe, warm, and understood.

Because, to him, it wasn't just about driving a bus; it was about being there when someone needed it most. And that was the best job he could ever ask for.

Every situation is different; every school and district has different policies and procedures. How cool would it be if a student had some tough issues going on and their bus driver decided to own the situation and tell the student "I got you" and walk with the student into the office. The driver would then let the school know the problem and shake the student's hand before returning to his/her bus. The bus driver has now made a relationship with this student who is more than likely to be a model student for the bus driver as long as they ride the bus. I want our public schools to be known for this type of customer service.

The role of a school bus driver extends beyond transportation; they are pivotal observers of students' well-being. Recognizing when a child is visibly distressed can lead to timely support, whether it's due to personal loss or family challenges. Having protocols to communicate such concerns can allow swift action, connecting the child with school counselors or relevant support staff. Imagine the positive impact when a bus driver takes the initiative to ensure a troubled student receives the necessary attention, reinforcing that the school is a supportive community. This level of care is what can set public schools apart, creating an environment where students feel genuinely supported.

Reflection/Discussion Questions

- What are some other ideas about how you could be an extra set of eyes for the students and/or the schools?

- Are students more likely to be on their best behavior for adults who show they care about them?

- What are some strategies you can utilize to help you keep up with current events going on within your school district that might impact riders on your bus?

- Do you think bus drivers should be trained on how to connect the various school district resources with children who have specific needs?

7

The Best Bus Drivers Know and Use Students' Names

> " Remember that a person's name is to that person the sweetest and most important sound in any language.[18]
> —Dale Carnegie, writer "

The finest bus drivers know the power of a name; they understand, as Dale Carnegie said, that a name can be a sweet sound to its owner.[19] Such recognition builds rapport and warmth, starting and ending the school day on a bright note. It's a simple act, calling a student by name, yet it resonates deeply, signaling care and attention that can turn a routine bus ride into an opportunity for connection.

Teachers and bus drivers who greet students by name often earn a special place in their hearts. It's a practice that resonates with students and parents alike, fostering an atmosphere of respect and community.

As superintendent, I happened to be walking through the schools and classrooms on the first day of school and I walked into a certain first-grade teacher's classroom. I immediately observed this teacher had made paper hats with name tags on them. This hat trick ensured her that she could address each child personally. Upon entering her classroom on this first day, I walked past a student's desk and read his hat "Hi, Edward," I said. "How are you today?" Edward looked up at me with such a confused look on his face and said, "How do you know my name?" He had already forgotten he was wearing a hat with his name on it! This story always brings a smile to my face as it is a positive example of a delightful implementation of my training.

Every morning at six fifteen sharp, Mrs. Harris started her bus route, the same one she had driven for the last twenty years. To her, it wasn't just about the driving. It was about the kids. She knew that, sometimes, a single smile or a simple "Good morning" could change the course of a kid's day. But her real secret weapon was learning every single student's name.

She didn't just memorize names; she made a point to know each kid's story. On their first ride of the year, she'd welcome them with a warm smile and ask, "What's your name, kiddo?" And then she'd follow up with something personal, like, "You play any sports?" or "What's your favorite thing to do after school?" It wasn't just small talk; it was her way of attaching their name to a piece of them.

If a new student hopped on the bus, looking a little lost or shy, she'd introduce herself right away. "Hey there! I'm Mrs. Harris.

What's your name?" As the kid told her, she'd nod thoughtfully, repeating it twice to cement it in her mind. Sometimes she'd even write it down on a small notepad she kept in her shirt pocket, jotting down any little detail that might help her remember—like "loves dinosaurs" or "wears red sneakers."

Mrs. Harris had a photographic memory when it came to faces, but she knew that remembering names took effort. She'd review her notes during her lunch break, recalling each student she'd met that morning, running their names through her head like a roll call. By the end of the first week, she'd know almost all of them by name, and by the end of the month, she'd know a little bit about who they were.

And it made a difference.

One chilly October morning, as the bus pulled up to its usual stop, a boy climbed on with his hood pulled tight over his head, eyes downcast. "Hey, Max!" Mrs. Harris greeted him, her voice warm. Max hesitated, his eyes lifting in surprise.

Mrs. Harris leaned down slightly, lowering her voice. "You doing okay? You're usually talking to your friends about baseball."

Max's eyes widened, the slightest smile tugging at his lips. "Just a rough morning," he muttered, but the fact that Mrs. Harris knew his name—and remembered something he liked—seemed to brighten his mood.

Later that day, a group of first graders clambered onto the bus, excitedly talking about a field trip they had just taken. "Hey, Ava!" Mrs. Harris called to a girl with braids. "Did you like the zoo today?"

Her eyes lit up. "Yes, Mrs. Harris! The lions were my favorite!"

"Lions, huh? Good choice," she said with a grin. She loved these little moments. Each name she spoke was like planting a small seed of connection, a reminder to each kid that someone knew they were there and cared enough to remember.

And when the holidays rolled around, Mrs. Harris had a little tradition. She'd bring small candy canes with each student's name attached in her neat handwriting. "For you, Lucy!" "Here you go, Jordan!" She'd make sure to personally hand each one out, using their names with a smile. It was her way of showing that even with a bus full of kids, she saw each one of them as an individual.

By the time students moved on to high school, Mrs. Harris knew she might not see them again, but she'd still wave if she spotted them walking to school or hanging out on their porches. And when she heard her name shouted from across the street—"Mrs. Harris!"—she knew her efforts to remember them had made a difference.

Because to Mrs. Harris, it wasn't just a bus route. It was a chance to make every kid feel seen, valued, and remembered. And sometimes, just hearing your name is enough to make a tough day a little brighter.

Imagine a bus driver mastering names with the help of a seating chart snapshot, creating a familiar environment from the get-go. This attention to detail, especially in pronouncing names correctly, is crucial, echoing respect and recognition during pivotal moments like graduations.

Reflecting on personal experiences and films like *Forrest Gump*, in the scene where Forrest is shunned on the bus, underscores the negative impact of exclusion. I've felt this, too, as a child riding various buses. The difference made by my compassionate driver, Mrs. Brown, who ensured inclusion and safety, was profound. It's this type of positive interaction and customer service that should be the hallmark of our public schools.

Reflection/Discussion Questions

- What are some ideas about how to quickly learn the names of the students on your bus?

- Is it a good idea to use the names of parents when you make contact with them?

- Have you ever had your name mispronounced or misspelled? How did it make you feel?

8

The Best Bus Drivers Let the Students Know a Little About Themselves

> " Vulnerability is the birthplace of empathy
> and deep connections.[20]
> —John Gottman, psychologist "

While we were conducting interviews for our second book and pouring through research, it became apparent that students' favorite adults had let the students know a little about themselves. This technique was something I learned during my first year of teaching in Eastern Kentucky. In one class where I was having trouble reaching some students, I mentioned that I used to work in tobacco to make some extra money. One student I had never connected with called me out on what he thought was a bluff. "Mr. Middleton, you always wear suits and a tie in school, and it is just hard to believe you ever worked in tobacco." A hush came over the room as this student never said much but was a leader with his particular group of farm kids.

Full disclosure, my time in tobacco fields was very limited but I could talk the talk. I said, "I used to cut about a thousand sticks a day and I dropped sticks from my shoulder, not like you soft kids who now drop them from a highboy."

The student was shocked, he perked up in class that very day, and not only was his attitude a lot better, but every student in the class picked up their level of interest in this class. This student started seeking me out to discuss farming, hunting, etc. He started bringing his friends around anytime he saw me in the hallway just to talk.

When teaching students, one learns the importance of embellishment. Honestly, I would have had trouble cutting a thousand sticks in a week! As farming conversations continued with students, there were times when I would call my father at night to tap his firsthand knowledge in order to keep the façade going. "Hey, Dad, what does it mean when tobacco comes into case?" Some may say that is being a little dishonest. I say I was connecting with students by finding common ground with them, and at the end of the day it improved both teaching and learning. Even though this was over thirty-six years ago, I can still remember those interactions as if they just occurred. You see, the students taught me a valuable life lesson that made me a better teacher and school administrator for the remainder of my career. It is easy to dislike someone you do not know and who you believe to be very different than yourself. Look for common ground and let others know a little about you if you want good, positive relationships.

About fifteen years ago, I was being interviewed by a school board and was asked the question, if you were hired, where would you live? I said I would live right in the middle of the community, eat at the local restaurants, and walk the streets where our students live. I believe that is one of the answers that caused this board to hire me. As I concluded my thirty-two-year tenure in this small community, the fact that I was viewed as a fellow community member rather than an outsider made a significant difference in how I was perceived and in the effectiveness of my role. Even when I made decisions that were unpopular in the community or when someone was not very fond of me, they were less likely to harbor animosity, recognizing that they at least knew a little about me and I cared enough to live in the same community.

Sparking Curiosity in Bus Riders

Jake had driven a school bus for fifteen years, shuttling kids to and from Rolling Pines Elementary. Most days were routine: he'd wave at parents, check his mirror, and count little heads as they shuffled to their seats. But one morning, as the last students boarded, he overheard a group of fourth graders chatting animatedly about their favorite teachers.

"Did you know Mrs. Beasley runs a dog rescue on weekends?" a boy named Tommy said, wide-eyed.

"Yeah! And Mr. Larson's a champion at tennis. He even showed us a trophy once!" chimed in Maria.

Jake was surprised by how much these kids knew about their teachers' lives outside the classroom. They seemed to connect with their teachers on a personal level, and he wondered what it might be like if the kids knew a little about him too.

Over the next week, Jake tested out subtle ways to share bits about himself. He started small. When he pulled up one chilly morning, he said, "Brrr! Reminds me of my school bus rides growing up. Back in my day, I had to wear thick mittens because there was no heater!" The kids giggled and, to his delight, asked him more questions. Did he ride the same kind of bus? What games did he play at recess? Soon, they were curious every day.

Jake decided to up his game. On Friday, he brought a small photo of himself from elementary school and pinned it next to the dashboard. "That's you, Mr. Jake?" a kindergartener asked, astonished. "Yep! And check out that vintage bus behind me!" He laughed. By now, the kids were eager to learn about his school days—cafeteria pizza and dodgeball included.

As the days rolled on, Jake found himself genuinely enjoying his job more than ever. The kids asked questions he'd never expect: How much did he have to study? Did he ever get in trouble? He even shared his love for classic rock, playing soft tunes during the ride to get them settled. To his surprise, the students responded positively. The usual chatter and rowdiness lessened, replaced by excited questions or quiet curiosity. The bus felt less like a chaotic shuttle and more like a moving community.

One morning, a fifth grader named Lily asked, "Mr. Jake, how'd you know you wanted to be a bus driver?" The question caught him off guard, but he answered honestly. He told them about his love for the road and for helping people get where they needed to be.

And he noticed that his bus, once just a job, had transformed into a place he couldn't wait to come back to each day.

One bus driver in one of my districts had posted a few pictures of himself and his family in the front of the bus for students to see. I really appreciated the driver finding a way to let the students know a little about him. Later, he told me that his supervisor told him he had to take the pictures down. The director said wind could enter the bus and send pictures flying into the face of the driver and then he might wreck the bus. I am sure the director found a bus law or regulation that backed up this decision. My only thought about this decision is if I had to "what if" every decision I made as a teacher, principal, and superintendent, I would be so frozen with fear that I would not have been able to do my job.

Reflection/Discussion Questions

- What are some examples of how you currently let students know a little about you?

- What are some ideas you are willing to try?

- How do other organizations let customers know a little about themselves?

9

The Best Bus Drivers Do Not Show Favoritism

The best bus drivers understand the importance of impartiality. Through my discussions with students over the years and during my book research, the theme of disliking favoritism emerged strongly. My years in education have shown me that the perceptions of favoritism can be as impactful as the act itself. It's essential to treat every student equitably and be mindful of how actions may be perceived.

For instance, consistently asking the same student to assist with tasks could be misinterpreted as preferential treatment.

Similarly, engaging only with athletes could signal favoritism. It's crucial to show equal interest in all students' activities. Experience has taught me to be aware of perceptions to avoid any undue impact on relationships within the school community. However, sometimes we just cannot control others' perceptions.

As a former school principal, if I visited one teacher's classroom more than the others', the perception was I either liked that teacher or he/she was about to be fired. Early in my administrative career as a middle school principal, one particular teacher, Bill, was a great teacher and student favorite. He and I became good friends. One year, the school district was getting rid of some very old computers. The computers had already been put up for surplus/auction and still no one wanted them, so they were then placed in the district dumpster. Bill saw them in the dumpster and went and pulled about six computers out. He then took them to his classroom and started trying to fix them. Bill went online to find people who still had old games for these computers. It is hard to say just how many hours Bill worked on these old computers that summer, but to his credit he had all of them up and running with the ability for his sixth-grade students to play fun, educational games on them. Before the school year began, I had teachers coming to see me about buying computers for their classrooms and I had to say no. They didn't like that. And when they saw that Bill had all these computers set up in his classroom, they got really jealous. Throughout the year, Bill said teachers made snide remarks about being the principal's favorite teacher. It got so bad Bill asked me to come down the hall and just find some reason to yell at him. So we staged for him to be out in the hallway during his class and I came toward him yelling at him for not being in the classroom. He tried to apologize, and

I just stayed on him. Later that night, Bill called and thanked me for the butt-chewing I gave him. Bill went on to tell me there had been a steady flow of teachers who made their way to his classroom to make sure he was okay. It was a great lesson for me early in my administrative career. I also learned that favoritism, or even the perception of favoritism, is hard on everyone.

The Bus Helper

Sandra had been driving her school bus route long enough to know most kids by name and habit. She cared about making things smooth for everyone, so when she noticed how the last students off the bus always left their windows down, she decided to create a new role: the *bus helper*. The bus helper's job would be simple: at the end of the ride, they'd go through and put up all the windows, leaving the bus neat and ready for the next morning. Sandra thought she'd solved her little problem efficiently.

The student she picked was Timmy, one of the last on her route and a kid she could count on to follow directions. But Sandra didn't anticipate how the rest of the kids would feel.

"Driver's pet!" they called Timmy as he walked to his seat the next day. Some kids rolled their eyes when they saw him take his "job" seriously, going from window to window with a sense of pride. Sandra saw it in the rearview mirror—the eye rolls, the muttering, and Timmy's flushed face as he tried to ignore it all. At first, Sandra brushed it off as regular kid stuff.

But the whispers got louder, the teasing more pointed. "You think you're special or something?" they'd say to Timmy, jabbing at his pride. The whole thing started to bother Sandra. Then, on her drive home one afternoon, she suddenly remembered her own school days.

Back in high school, Sandra, who didn't play any sports, remembered that the teachers had always gone easier on the athletes. They got away with things the rest couldn't. That feeling of favoritism used to sting. The memory hit her hard, reminding her that even if she hadn't meant it, choosing one kid as her helper had created a kind of divide. She decided to make a change.

The next morning, as the kids piled onto the bus, Sandra addressed them. "Hey, everyone! So, about those windows—I'm going to switch things up a bit," she said with a smile. "We're going to do a rotation. Every day, I'll pick someone new to help with the windows, or maybe we can all make sure to check our own on the way out." The kids perked up; a few even smiled. And Sandra could tell that the simple tweak had taken the spotlight off Timmy.

The new system worked. Sandra made sure each kid got a turn, and soon enough, the teasing stopped. Timmy seemed relieved, his face no longer downcast, and the bus felt friendlier. Sandra learned to keep an eye out for anything that might feel unfair, real or imagined. Her bus had become more than a ride home— it was a little community where every kid contributed and knew that they mattered.

It was no different being in the central office or being superintendent. If I went out to one school more than the others, staff thought that was my favorite school and my favorite principal. If I ate lunch in one cafeteria and not the others, they assumed I thought the cooks in one school were better at cooking meals. If these *adults* are so in tune with favoritism, then we know that the *students* on each bus are always looking to see if everyone is treated equitably by the driver. Students express a true fondness for adults who treat everyone equally, so fairness on the bus is a must.

Reflection/Discussion Questions

- Have you ever felt a teacher or boss had favorites and you were not one of them?

- Have you ever been considered a favorite by a teacher or boss? How did it make you feel? How did others react?

- What are some of the things we do that might make students feel like we have favorites?

- Do we all have favorites? What are some of the best ways to avoid even the perception of favoritism?

10

The Best Bus Drivers Recover Well When Mistakes Are Made

> **"** The greatest mistake you can make in life is to be continually fearing you will make one.[22]
> —Elbert Hubbard, writer **"**

I was a freshman in high school, enrolled in a class I had little interest in. Still, I was behaving well and doing just enough to maintain a solid "B." One day, the teacher asked to see me after class. He explained that he was missing some photographs, and that another student had told him I had been looking at them. This teacher also happened to be the school and local newspaper photographer.

I told him honestly that I had never seen the pictures and thought to myself, *Why would I even be interested in them?* Had the conversation ended there, it probably wouldn't have been memorable. But it didn't.

He kept pushing—clearly assuming I was guilty. It was obvious he didn't believe me. I remember saying, "Why would I want to take your pictures?" But he wouldn't let up, and eventually, I just walked away.

That conversation took place over forty-five years ago, and I still remember it vividly. What's more, I've never forgiven him for accusing me of stealing. After that day, I mentally checked out of his class. I did just enough to earn a "C," but I stopped participating entirely. I refused to engage with him for the rest of my freshman year.

Worse yet, I carried that grudge beyond the classroom. I avoided him at after-school events during my remaining three years of high school. I never spoke well of him to friends. Even years later, after graduation, I saw him in public and still refused to acknowledge him.

Looking back now, I realize it wouldn't have taken much to change everything. If he had simply apologized—if he had told me he didn't really believe I was a thief—I could have moved on. I might have even respected him. But without that apology, the damage has lingered for forty-five years.

If I had to pick one of the customer service concepts that we struggle with most in education, it would be admitting mistakes. When I spoke with students in my research, they repeatedly said their favorite adults admit when they make mistakes.[23] In Ken Blanchard's research, he found that it is *better* to make mistakes and recover well than to never make mistakes in the first place.[24] What an interesting concept! I'll go into more detail about that later in this chapter.

> Unhappy customers typically tell nine people about their negative experiences.[25] That's some really bad word of mouth!

Early in my teaching career, I had a student who was giving me a very tough time each day in class. One day he actually mouthed off to me in front of the whole class and I asked him to see me in my office. During this meeting, I got up in the student's face and physically challenged him. I am not proud of this moment, and had the student made an aggressive move, I probably would have done something that would have caused me to lose my job. The student backed down and left my office. My actions bothered me the remainder of that day and even through the night. I felt horrible. The next day I smiled at him in the hallway and asked to see him in my office again. He was a little hesitant, but I assured him it would be okay. I apologized to this student and told him I was wrong. I even said perhaps I could do a better job teaching as I was clearly not reaching him. I asked him a few questions about himself and told him a few things about myself. We actually had a few things in common. We laughed, shook hands, and he left my office. I felt so much better after getting that off my chest. The change in this student's behavior was amazing. He started working in my class every day and many times would just come up and start talking with me before class, after class, and during lunch. The small act of admitting my mistake made a tremendous difference in my relationship with this student and may have saved my career.

As humans, we are going to make mistakes. We can deny them, try to cover them up, or just own up to the mistake. In my research, I found that some teachers even made mistakes *on purpose* during the first days of school so that they could admit them to their students and maybe get a laugh too.[26] These teachers told me they wanted students to take chances and not be afraid to make mistakes in their classes. Is it any wonder these teachers were thought to be the best in the eyes of their students?

Have you ever made mistakes driving a school bus? Here is a list of possible scenarios that you may have encountered or heard about.

Have you ever . . .

- dinged another vehicle?

- knocked off another driver's mirror?

- missed a student on a bus route?

- driven onto someone's yard and caused damage?

- called a student by the wrong name or mispronounced a name?

- had a bad day and taken it out on a student?

- made a mistake with a coworker or boss?

As a leader, when one of my employees admits mistakes and apologizes, the situation always goes better for both of us. Once someone admits the mistake, what else is there for a leader to say? On the other hand, if a driver denies doing anything wrong, tries to cover it up, or lies about what happened, I would have to seriously consider if they were going to continue to be employed at my school. Owning up to your mistakes can save your job. I'll explain just how to give the best apology in the next section.

The Steps to a Great Apology

A few years ago, I was dating a woman named Amy, who would soon become my second wife. Amy is not part of the education world so when she had a school bus issue, she asked me to help. I was a retiring school superintendent, and even though I had already written five books on school customer service, this problem was tricky because it was not in my school district.

Our area had seen a lot of snow during that winter, and snow covered her yard and driveway. The bus that had picked up Amy's daughter had driven up on Amy's front lawn and left some really bad tire marks in the grass.

So Amy called the bus garage and left them a message about what happened, but never heard back from the garage. Then she came to me and told me about the situation. When I heard about the damage the driver did to her lawn and the transportation department completely ignoring her calls, I knew that how the school responded to this big mistake would determine how Amy saw the school system as a whole moving forward.

I happened to be friends with the superintendent in this district, and I knew he was all about customer service. I had Amy take pictures of her yard and email them to the superintendent. In a matter of a few days, she received a phone call with a sincere apology for the damage and their unresponsiveness, and a landscaping company came to her home and fixed her front yard.

Mistakes can be a very positive thing if handled correctly. As I mentioned earlier, Ken Blanchard says it is better to make a mistake and recover well than to never make a mistake at all.[27] When makes are made, there are three key elements to the best recovery:

1. Apologize as quickly as possible. The longer you wait to apologize, the harder it is for the person to believe you mean it.
2. Have empathy when you apologize. Try to put yourself in the shoes of your customer and make sure it is sincere.
3. Try your best to make your apology be as good as the problem you caused. In other words, try to make the apology be equal to the offense.

Let's look at the story above. Did the school demonstrate these three factors? Yes. After Amy did not receive a call back, the superintendent took it into his own hands to fix this error. He immediately called and offered a gracious apology. So number one and two above were met. The superintendent quickly mobilizing a team to fix her lawn showed that the superintendent was willing to fix his school's mistake.

Later that year, I was attending a superintendent function and Amy decided to join me. It just so happened that the superintendent who had fixed her yard was there, too. When I pointed him out to Amy, she jumped up from the table and went right over to him. She said she was a parent in his district and introduced herself. I could tell he was a tad nervous about what Amy was about to say in front of his peers, as we don't normally hear positive feedback in our positions.

However, Amy started *thanking* him for the job he was doing in his school district. She specifically talked about the college prep program where her daughter was receiving college credits during her senior year. My superintendent friend, I swear he grew four inches when he heard her, enjoying the praise, especially as his peers were listening. Amy never mentioned about having her yard fixed.

This one mistake started an entirely new friendship between Amy and that superintendent, and he was able to create what Ken Blanchard calls a "raving fan!"[28] Ken Blanchard coined the term "raving fan" to describe a customer who is so overwhelmed and floored by the customer service they've received that they can't stop telling everyone about it. This one mistake actually turned into several positive outcomes for the superintendent and his school district.

As a side note, later that night, I took great delight in telling the superintendent that he could thank me for that public recognition he received. When he realized Amy was my wife and that she was the one whose lawn he'd fixed, we had a good laugh together. We actually became close friends, and he would even attend our wedding celebration.

A few years later, after my retirement, I received a call that I had won the Lifetime Achievement Award in the Northern Kentucky area. After investigating who was on this committee, I found out it was the very same superintendent. Had I not told Amy to email him and had he not fixed Amy's yard, she wouldn't have had reason to brag on him at the superintendent event, and I doubt I would have been selected to achieve this prestigious award. Giving great customer service can provide amazing results . . . some of which you may never even expect!

A Mistake Turned Opportunity

Consider this hypothetical scenario. You drive a bus for the ACME school district, and it is the first day of school. You forget about one of the families on your route and thus do not pick up little Johnny and Susan. As you are on your way home, you receive a call from the bus garage telling you about your mistake. The transportation secretary lets you know the parents are furious and asks that you please not miss this family tomorrow.

If you believe in providing great customer service, how do you handle a similar situation? Remember the three steps to a great apology. What about calling the parents and apologizing to them as soon as possible? That's the immediate apology you're looking to make. Let them know you will also apologize to Johnny and Susan when you bring them home today. Maybe mention how it must have felt lonely or scary for them that the bus never came. That shows you have empathy for the family. What about stopping by the house and apologizing face-to-face? Maybe try to talk a while and get to know the parents. You could then give them your business card as a way to contact you directly the next time there is an issue. Now your apology has equaled the offense. Additionally, you may have just created a "raving fan" instead of having two mad parents working against you for the rest of the year.

These three steps to a great apology work in both your professional and personal life. People understand that we all make mistakes. The problems arise when we try to cover up the mistake, blame others, or make excuses. Learning how to apologize should make you a little more relaxed when it comes to making a mistake. Instead of getting all worried about the mistake, perhaps we should start thinking of mistakes as opportunities.

Reflection/Discussion Questions

- Can you think of a mistake you have made where you did not recover well? Explain.

- Can you think of a mistake you have made where you did recover well? Explain.

- Can you think of a mistake that a celebrity has made and give reasons why the recovery either worked for the person or did not work for the person?

11

The Best Bus Drivers Are in Control of Their Bus

> We are faced with an important question,
> 'Who's driving your bus?'
> —Unknown

I've observed hundreds of bus drivers over the years and sat in on more disciplinary meetings than I can count—some resulting in suspensions or even terminations. Most of these cases shared a common thread: the driver had lost control of the bus. That is, students were unruly, ignored instructions, and created an atmosphere that made the ride unpleasant—or even unsafe—for everyone on board.

I've watched plenty of bus footage from our schools. There have been more instances than I'd like to admit of bus drivers losing control of their buses. I'm honestly grateful some of it never ended up on YouTube, TikTok, or CNN. That said, I've also witnessed the opposite: drivers delivering what I'd call "gold standard" customer service—balancing friendliness with firm control. In my view, a driver might be liked by students, but if they want to be respected, they must maintain order.

When interviewing students about their favorite teachers, one theme surfaced again and again: the best teachers ran orderly classrooms with consistent discipline. Students told me they actually wanted rules. They appreciated structure—and expected everyone, including the teacher, to follow the rules. Sure, they might still like teachers who were more laid-back, but the ones they respected most always maintained control.

When I was in fourth grade, I transferred to a county school in Orangeburg, Kentucky. Every day, I rode about forty-five minutes to and from school on Mrs. Brown's big yellow bus. This was in the late sixties and early seventies—long before there were cameras or bus monitors.

Mrs. Brown transported a mix of elementary through high school students, and she ruled her bus with an iron fist. All it took was a glance in her mirror, and instant silence would ripple through the bus. I still remember being able to see the whites of her eyes, even from the back seat of the bus. When I boarded each day, she'd speak to me first, and I'd return the greeting. Then I'd quietly find my seat, moving as carefully and respectfully as someone approaching the Soup Nazi's counter on *Seinfeld*.[29]

To some, that might sound extreme. But as a young student, I appreciated the order. No one dared to mess with Mrs. Brown. She had a reputation, and it kept things in line. In the three years I rode her bus, I never once saw a fight or witnessed anyone seriously challenge her authority.

Riding with Mrs. Brown didn't come with a lot of warm fuzzies—but parents wanted their kids on that bus. Why? Because it was safe. Because it was calm. And because it was bully-free. And for us students, that sense of safety meant everything. I never had to worry about what might happen on the way to or from school—not as long as Mrs. Brown was behind the wheel.

The Enforcer, Mrs. Malone

In a small town nestled in the hills, there was a school bus driver named Mrs. Kathy Malone. She wasn't just any bus driver—she was a guardian, a leader, and a role model, all rolled into one. Her route, bus twenty-three, was legendary among students and parents alike. Known for her firm but fair demeanor, Mrs. Malone was the driver that every parent requested for their child, and every student respected. Riding bus twenty-three wasn't just about getting from home to school—it was a journey of respect, order, and kindness.

Mrs. Malone's secret? She had high expectations and a keen eye for fairness. There was no nonsense on bus twenty-three. From the moment students stepped onto the bus, they knew the rules and they knew she meant business. No pushing, no yelling, no roughhousing. She insisted that students scoot over when a seat was shared, and she made sure that no one, no matter their grade, was left standing or isolated. "We're all family on this bus," she'd say with a warm smile, and she meant it.

One chilly morning, a new student named Danny, a shy fourth grader, boarded the bus, nervously looking around. He spotted an open seat next to a couple of older boys who were known for their loud jokes and rough play. When one of them tried to crowd Danny out of the seat, Mrs. Malone's voice boomed from the driver's seat, "Boys, make room—everyone deserves a seat." With a slight blush, the boys immediately shifted over, and Danny sat down with a relieved smile.

Then there was little Emma, a first grader with a mop of curly hair who had once been teased by older girls for her big glasses. Mrs. Malone had put a stop to it swiftly. The next morning, she handed Emma a small sticker with a bright smiley face, telling her, "You're braver than you think, Emma. Wear those glasses with pride!" From then on, those older girls became her unofficial protectors—Mrs. Malone somehow shifted their perspective from teasing to defending. It was magic and it was just her way.

Parents praised Mrs. Malone's no-nonsense approach, and stories circulated about her dedication to keeping every child safe. Mrs. Rodriguez, mother of two sons on bus twenty-three, often said, "If Mrs. Malone sees a problem, it's solved before it starts. My boys know that respect comes first on that bus."

For some students, Mrs. Malone's bus even felt more structured and comfortable than their classrooms. "I actually like the bus better than some of my classes," admitted Sarah, a middle schooler. "Mrs. Malone treats us with respect, and she expects us to be respectful too. No one messes around when she's in charge."

Mrs. Malone's reputation grew, and so did the list of parents who requested bus twenty-three for their children. She wasn't just driving kids to school, she was giving them a lesson in kindness, discipline, and mutual respect every single day. As for Mrs. Malone, she would simply smile when people praised her, gently reminding them, "It's a team effort. I just set the rules, and the kids make me proud by following them."

Being in control of your bus benefits you and your riders. It can be hard sometimes to enforce rules or crack down on kids having fun, especially since they're not in a learning environment and there's only so much they can do to occupy their minds on a school bus. But a little work up front, at the beginning of the school year, will set the tone for the rest of the year and make the ride more enjoyable for everyone.

Reflection/Discussion Questions

- Think back to your school days as a student. Did you have any bus drivers who were not in control of their bus? What was it like to ride the bus?

- Did you ever have a classroom teacher who did not have control of the classroom? How is this similar to a school bus where the driver does not have control of his/her school bus?

- Did you have any bus drivers who had good discipline on their bus? How did this make you feel?

- In your opinion, what do bus drivers with great discipline do differently?

12

The Best Bus Drivers Tell Students Why

" Knowledge shared is knowledge squared.
—Unknown "

As a parent and a grandparent, I am used to hearing young children ask "why" multiple times when they are told to do something. I am guilty of not using research as I blurt out, "Because I said so." I know good and well that is not the proper way to get compliance from someone, whether it's my two-year-old grandchild or an adult who has driven a school bus for over thirty years. When we interviewed students, they told us they just like to know "why" when they are asked to do something.[30]

When asked to do something by a boss, do you like to know the reason behind the request? I remember when our district was switching to direct deposit for all employees. We had some bus drivers who were so upset they were threatening to quit. Had we spent more time talking to our drivers and monitors about why this was important and how they would receive their checks at least one day earlier, the transition would have been much smoother. After a few months of implementation, drivers realized they did not have to worry about losing their checks, and this cut down on their trips to the bank. No special trips in the summer to pick up their checks, no more being absent on check day and not being able to pick up their check, etc. Had we covered all this with our drivers before the mandate, we would have saved so much time. While we may not have said "Because I said so," our actions certainly did. At the end of the day, babies going through their terrible twos and adults ready to retire all like to know why when being asked to do something.

John Maxwell, a renowned leadership author, suggests that relying on authority is the most basic form of leadership, and one that cannot be held for long if leaders want to have success.[31] My own research supports this, indicating that the best educators are those who provide a rationale for their requests.[32] It stands to reason that explaining the "why"—for instance, asking students to close bus windows with a reason like avoiding a wet seat the next day if it rains—increases compliance. The word "because" is powerful, and its use can foster a better response from both students and adults alike.

"Why" in Action

Knowing the Why

It was a regular Friday afternoon on Mrs. Johnson's bus, filled with chatter and the usual excitement for the weekend ahead. Mrs. Johnson was driving her usual route, smiling as she heard snippets of conversations. But what set Mrs. Johnson apart was her habit of always explaining the "why" behind her rules.

For weeks, she had reminded the students why they needed to keep the aisles clear, put their bags under the seats, and stay seated with their seat belts on. "If there's ever an emergency," she would say, "we need to be able to move quickly and safely off the bus." Most days, the students would nod, listening respectfully, even if they didn't fully understand. It seemed like just another rule. Until the day everything changed.

The Moment of Crisis

That Friday, as the bus made its way down a quiet country road, Mrs. Johnson noticed something unusual. A car was speeding toward them, swerving uncontrollably. In an instant, she realized it was going to crash right into the side of the bus.

"Brace yourselves!" Mrs. Johnson shouted. The impact was sudden and jarring. The car collided with the side of the bus, pushing it into a ditch. The bus tilted to one side but didn't roll over. The kids screamed, but no one was hurt. The training kicked in for Mrs. Johnson, and she quickly assessed the situation. The bus was stuck, but it wasn't safe to stay put—there was smoke coming from the engine.

The Escape Plan

"Listen up, everyone!" Mrs. Johnson called out, her voice calm and steady despite the chaos. "We need to get off the bus, and we need to do it fast. Remember what I've told you—leave your bags, stay in line, and move quickly to the front door."

The students sprang into action, almost as if they had practiced this a hundred times before. No one hesitated. They knew exactly why they needed to leave their belongings and keep the aisles clear. They moved swiftly, one by one, holding onto the handrails as Mrs. Johnson directed them out of the bus.

Outside, they gathered a safe distance away, exactly as Mrs. Johnson had taught them. A few of the younger kids were crying, but the older students comforted them, knowing that they had done everything right.

The Aftermath

Within minutes, emergency vehicles arrived. The firefighters quickly assessed the situation, and one of them, a tall man in a yellow helmet, approached Mrs. Johnson.

"You did everything perfectly," he said, nodding in approval. "Getting everyone off so fast—that smoke could've turned into a fire."

Mrs. Johnson smiled, but she turned to the kids, her eyes filled with pride. "You all saved yourselves today," she said. "You remembered why we have these rules, and you followed them without a second thought."

Tyler, one of the older boys, stepped forward. "We knew what to do because you always explained it to us," he said. "We understood why, so we didn't panic." Mrs. Johnson felt a lump in her throat. She had always believed in the power of the "why," but seeing it in action, knowing it had made a difference, was overwhelming.

A Lesson for Life

As the parents arrived to pick up their children, they hugged Mrs. Johnson tightly, thanking her for keeping their kids safe. But Mrs. Johnson knew it wasn't just her—it was the kids who had listened, who had understood the reasons behind her rules.

From that day on, whenever Mrs. Johnson explained the "why" behind a rule, the students listened with a newfound respect. They knew that sometimes understanding the reason wasn't just about following directions—it could be the difference between panic and safety, between chaos and order.

And as the bus pulled away the following Monday, with everyone safely in their seats and the aisles clear, Mrs. Johnson felt a deep sense of gratitude. The kids didn't just know the rules—they knew the why. And that had saved their lives.

Examples of "Why" on the School Bus

Here are some practical examples of a bus driver explaining the "why" behind rules or requests to students, making the rationale clear to encourage better behavior and compliance.

1. Seat Belts and Staying Seated

Instead of simply saying, "Keep your seat belt on and stay seated," Mrs. Johnson might say: "I need everyone to keep their seat belts on and stay seated because if I have to stop quickly, it will keep you safe and prevent you from getting hurt. The seat belt helps protect you, just like it does in a car."

Why It Works: By explaining that the rule is about safety, students understand that it's not arbitrary; it's there to protect them from harm. This can make them more likely to comply, especially if they recognize the reason.

2. No Loud Talking or Yelling

Instead of just saying, "No yelling on the bus," Mrs. Johnson might say: "Please keep your voices down because if I can't hear the traffic and the sounds outside, it's harder for me to drive safely. I need to be able to focus to make sure we all get to school without any problems."

Why It Works: This explanation helps students see that their actions directly affect the driver's ability to keep them safe, making the rule feel more logical and reasonable.

3. Assigned Seating

If Mrs. Johnson assigns specific seats, rather than saying, "Sit where I tell you," she might explain, "I've given you assigned seats because it helps me know where everyone is, which makes it easier to check that everyone got on safely. It also helps prevent arguments, so we can have a smoother ride."

Why It Works: By clarifying that the assigned seating is meant to ensure safety and reduce conflicts, students are more likely to accept the arrangement.

4. Keeping Aisles Clear

Instead of saying, "Put your bags under the seat," Mrs. Johnson might say: "Please keep the aisles clear by putting your bags under the seat because if there's an emergency, we need to be able to get off the bus quickly without tripping over anything."

Why It Works: This explanation ties the rule to emergency preparedness, which emphasizes the importance of the rule beyond simple tidiness.

5. No Throwing Objects

If Mrs. Johnson notices students tossing items, she could say: "I need you to keep your hands and belongings to yourself because if something hits another student or distracts me while I'm driving, it could cause an accident. We all want to get home safely."

Why It Works: This connects the request to the potential consequences of their actions, making it clear that the rule isn't about limiting fun but about everyone's safety.

6. Waiting to Stand Up Until the Bus Stops

Instead of saying, "Don't get up until the bus stops," Mrs. Johnson might explain: "Please wait until the bus comes to a complete stop before standing up because if the bus moves suddenly while you're standing, you could fall and get hurt."

Why It Works: By giving a concrete reason related to student safety, it reinforces the importance of the rule and helps students understand the potential risks.

7. Putting the Windows Up Before Exiting the Bus

"Before you get off the bus, please remember to put your window up if you're the last one sitting there. If the window is left down and it rains overnight, your seat will be soaking wet tomorrow morning, and no one wants to start the day sitting in a puddle!"

Why It Works: This explanation connects the action (putting the window up) to a direct, relatable consequence (having to sit in a wet seat). It helps students see that the rule isn't just for the bus driver's convenience—it's actually for their own comfort.

Conclusion

These examples show how providing students with the reason behind a rule or request can make them more likely to comply. When students understand the "why," it gives them a sense of the bigger picture and helps them see that the rules are there for their well-being, not just to control their behavior. This approach builds respect, trust, and cooperation, making the bus ride smoother and safer for everyone.

Reflection/Discussion Questions

- Do our supervisors do a good job of telling us why we are being asked to do certain requirements of our jobs? If no, how could communication be improved?

- Give some examples of requests we give to students on our bus and then give the why behind the request. Hint: Saying "because I said so" is not an appropriate response.

- How does the staff in a school district react when given a new task without any explanation? Does it seem fair to do the same to students?

13

The Best Bus Drivers Have a Clean School Bus

> " Cleanliness and order are not matters of instinct; they are matters of education, and like most great things, you must cultivate a taste for them.[33]
> —Benjamin Disraeli,
> former British Prime Minister "

Have you ever decided to use a particular gas station just because they have a cleaner restroom? Buc-ee's, the Texas-based chain, and Dunkin' Donuts, the New England-based chain, are notorious for having clean restrooms. The best businesses, whether they're gas stations, restaurants, or even car shares like Uber or Lyft, have a clean appearance. They know that what you see right when you enter goes a long way. It's a first impression that lasts.

The Coffee Stain Study

One of my favorite stories in marketing is the "Coffee Stain Study" that was conducted by Braniff Airlines years and years ago when they were a major airline.[34] They had several brand-new airplanes and they brought future passengers on to experience them. They asked the passengers to rate the company on areas like quality of service, safety, food quality, on-time arrivals/departures, and overall safety. The passengers would pull down the tray tables, look at the vents, and they would rate *the whole experience* just from what they could see from their seats. It sounds crazy, but there's a reason for this.

For the study, the airline brought one group on board to experience a perfectly clean plane and had them rate the airline. They then brought in the next group, but before they came in, the airline went to every other row and put a coffee stain on the inside of the tray table. Nothing else changed.

In the group that had the coffee stain on the tray table, one striking similarity stuck out—all the marks consistently across the board, from service, food quality, and on-time arrival to overall safety, were lower than the group that had no coffee stain. Imagine that! Such a wild swing of far-reaching impressions just from one small detail.

"Cleanliness is next to godliness."

This study has much to do with our perceptions and, as I like to say in the customer service world, *perceptions are reality*.

Would you rather ride in a clean car or a dirty car? What about a taxi? What if you use Uber and the driver pulls up in an old car that needs to be washed and as you get into the car the seats are torn with graffiti written on them, the windows are dirty, and the driver is dressed in worn, dirty jeans and a tank top? Would you still use this Uber? Or feel comfortable during your ride?

The Impact of a Clean Bus on Student Experience

In the small, tightly knit community of Maplewood, the school district's transportation department had long been a source of frustration for students and parents alike. The buses were old, often dirty, and poorly maintained. Graffiti adorned the seats, trash littered the floors, and unpleasant odors greeted riders every morning. Many students dreaded the bus ride, and parents grumbled about the lack of care and professionalism. The buses became a symbol of the district's neglect, tarnishing its reputation.

They decided to hire a new driver who had worked in a different school district before recently moving to Maplewood. Mr. Anderson was a seasoned bus driver known for his unwavering commitment to maintaining a spotless bus. Each morning, before embarking on his route, he cleaned both the interior and exterior of his bus. The floors gleamed, the seats were free of debris, and the windows wiped clean, offering students a clear view of their journey.

Very quickly, sentiments changed in the community. Students eagerly awaited Mr. Anderson's bus, often commenting on its pristine condition. "I love riding Mr. Anderson's bus; it always feels so welcoming," remarked Jenna, a fifth grader. The clean environment fostered a sense of pride and respect among the students. They were more inclined to keep the bus tidy, refraining from littering or causing damage.

Teachers and parents noticed a positive shift in the students' behavior. Mrs. Lopez, a teacher at Maplewood Elementary, observed, "Students arriving on Mr. Anderson's bus are more punctual and exhibit a positive attitude throughout the day." Parents appreciated the safe and clean environment their children experienced daily.

Mr. Anderson's dedication did not go unnoticed by the school administration. They recognized that his efforts contributed significantly to the students' well-being and the overall perception of the school's transportation services. His clean bus became a symbol of care and excellence within the community.

This narrative underscores the profound impact that a clean vehicle can have on passengers, especially students. A well-maintained bus not only enhances comfort but also fosters respect, responsibility, and a positive outlook among its riders.

Our customers deserve a nice, clean bus, with seats in good condition and without cuss words written on them. How can we ask students to take pride in our school and district if the bus drivers do not take pride in their buses?

A Vision for Change

Mr. Anderson inspired the transportation director, Ms. Clara, to implement some of his best practices into the rules and responsibilities of the district's bus drivers. She made her vision clear to her team: "We are not just bus drivers; we are ambassadors for our schools. Our buses are rolling classrooms, and every ride should reflect the same pride and care as the schools themselves." Every bus, Ms. Clara declared, must be immaculate both inside and out. Her plan included:

1. **Daily Inspections:** Each driver was required to inspect their bus at the end of every route. Seats were checked for graffiti or damage, floors were swept, and trash bins emptied. Any issues were reported and addressed immediately.

2. **Weekly Deep Cleaning:** A schedule was established for all buses to undergo thorough cleaning, including shampooing the seats, washing the walls and windows, and deodorizing the interiors.

3. **Exterior Maintenance:** Buses were washed weekly, ensuring they gleamed as they traveled through the community. Ms. Clara believed that a clean, shiny bus conveyed professionalism and pride.

4. **Rapid Repairs:** A maintenance team was on standby to repair any issues, from broken seat belts to torn upholstery, within twenty-four hours of being reported.

5. **Driver Engagement:** Drivers attended workshops on professionalism and were encouraged to take ownership of their buses. Ms. Clara reminded them, "A clean bus isn't just about appearances—it's about

creating a safe and respectful environment for our students."

6. **Student and Parent Partnerships:** Ms. Clara involved students and parents in the transformation. She organized a "Bus Pride Week," inviting families to tour the newly cleaned buses and discuss the changes. Students were encouraged to report issues and rewarded for respecting the buses.

The Impact

At first, the changes were met with skepticism. Parents doubted the initiative would last, and students doubted anyone cared enough to enforce the new rules. But over time, the results spoke for themselves.

- **A New Experience for Students:** Each morning, students boarded buses that smelled fresh, looked spotless, and felt inviting. The graffiti was gone, the seats were intact, and every bus was a welcoming space. Students began respecting the buses, keeping them clean and reporting damage.

- **Pride in the Fleet:** Parents noticed the gleaming buses on the roads and were impressed by the district's commitment. A parent named Mr. Haynes remarked, "I used to drive my kids to school because I didn't want them riding those old, dirty buses. Now, they can't wait to hop on each morning!"

- **A Shift in Culture:** The changes extended beyond the buses. Teachers reported that students arrived at school in better moods and were less agitated from their morning commute. Parents began praising the district on social media, calling the transformation "inspiring" and "long overdue."

- **Community Recognition:** Local news outlets caught wind of the changes, highlighting the transformation as a symbol of what strong leadership and community collaboration could achieve. The district even received awards for innovation and excellence in transportation.

A Lasting Legacy

One day, a student named Jamie stood up during a school assembly and addressed the crowd. "When the buses got cleaner, I felt like we mattered more," Jamie said. "It showed that people care about us. And now, I'm proud to say I ride the bus."

Mr. Anderson sat in the audience, a tear in his eye. His work wasn't just about buses; it was about fostering respect, pride, and a sense of belonging in every student who stepped onto a Maplewood school bus.

The once-dreaded yellow buses became a symbol of excellence and care, not just for the transportation department, but for the entire district. Thanks to Ms. Clara's leadership and determination, the Maplewood School District's reputation was forever changed—for the better.

Reflection/Discussion Questions

- Have you ever chosen to use a particular gas station based on the cleanliness of their restroom? Why or why not?

- Did you ever leave a place of business or choose another location because a particular place was just too dirty?

- Do you feel better about using an Uber that is clean on both the outside and inside of the vehicle? Can you name some businesses that are usually clean and some that are usually dirty?

- We know that a great first impression is very important. Can cleanliness help you make a great first impression? Explain your answer.

14

The Best Bus Drivers Walk in the Shoes of Their Students

" You can't lead someone to a place
you've never been.[35]
—Rod Rogers, pastor "

The best public school bus drivers walk in the shoes of their customers. What does that mean? Often, it means putting yourself in your students' situation and feeling what they feel. Another word for this is empathy. When we walk in the shoes of the students, we can see a situation from their perspective and can empathize with how they may feel about it. Bus drivers who have empathy for their students can forge stronger bonds with their passengers.

Some alarming statistics:

- One in five students has at least one parent who struggles with alcoholism.

- Seven percent (one in fourteen students) live with a grandparent.

- One in nine girls and one in eighteen boys have been sexually abused or assaulted.

- One in seven children boarded your bus hungry: eleven million children in this country are living in "food-insecure" homes.

Assume you pick up sixty students on your bus route. Given these statistics and assuming there are no overlapping issues, nine of your riders are hungry, twelve riders have an alcoholic parent, four riders live with a grandparent, and six of the girls on your bus have been sexually abused along with three boys. Having been a public-school teacher and administrator for thirty-two years, I have listened to people bad-mouth public schools and talk negatively about student behavior. Given the statistics above, I believe students do a great job showing up for school and giving us their best. The best bus drivers understand that many students face terrible home lives, and many will board their bus tired, hungry, and abused. *By knowing these facts, we all should have empathy for our customers who spend eight to ten hours with us before they must return home to a very unstable environment.* I am not saying by being empathetic we lower our expectations; I am saying do not take it personally if a student is having a bad day. The empathetic bus driver might be the only positive experience a student has all day.

These statistics are sobering and highlight the diverse and often challenging backgrounds from which students come. Bus drivers are often the first adults kids see in the morning and the last ones they see before heading home. These brief interactions might not seem like a big deal, but for a lot of students, it really is. Some of them are coming from tough situations we may never fully know about, and the way we treat them can make a huge difference.

Being kind, calm, and consistent on the bus might be one of the few predictable parts of a student's day. That simple routine, paired with a smile or a friendly word, can help create a sense of safety and stability. And when a kid acts out or seems off? It's worth remembering that their behavior might be about something much bigger than the bus ride. It's not personal. Keeping that perspective can help you respond with patience instead of frustration.

For some students, just having a supportive adult around—someone who sees them and treats them with respect—is a game changer. Those little moments of connection can build trust over time, and that trust opens the door for real communication. Sometimes, a student just needs to know that someone cares.

Of course, being supportive doesn't mean we take on everything ourselves. If something serious is going on, it's important to share that concern with the right people at school. Boundaries matter, too—we can be caring and professional at the same time.

In the end, it's about showing up with empathy. A little understanding can go a long way, and you never know how much of a difference your presence might be making in a student's life.

Mr. Ray's Ride: How One Bus Driver Changed a Life

Every morning, Mr. Ray drove bus twenty-two through the quiet streets of Elmwood. He knew every turn, every stop, and every child's name. But one student stood out: Susie Parker, a quiet sixth-grader who always sat alone in the middle row, her head down, eyes fixed on her worn-out sneakers.

Seeing Through the Silence

Mr. Ray had a sharp eye for more than just traffic. He noticed how Susie avoided talking to other kids, how her clothes were often the same as the day before, and how her lunch box was often empty when she opened it after school. He could see she was struggling, though she never said a word.

How could your district improve bus driver training? What characteristics should your district look for when recruiting and hiring bus drivers?

One morning, after Susie climbed aboard and slipped into her usual seat, Mr. Ray gently said, "Good morning, Susie. Those sneakers look like they've seen some adventures." Surprised, she managed a shy smile and nodded. It was a small crack in the wall she had built around herself, but Mr. Ray knew even the smallest opening could make a difference.

Walking in Her Shoes

Mr. Ray remembered his own childhood—growing up in a tough neighborhood, wearing hand-me-down clothes, and knowing what it felt like to be invisible. He decided he wouldn't let Susie feel that way anymore.

He started by making the bus a welcoming space. Every morning, he greeted her warmly and saved her favorite seat near the front. He introduced "Question of the Day," a lighthearted trivia game, always making sure Susie got a chance to answer. Slowly, she started participating, even laughing sometimes.

Going the Extra Mile

One particularly cold winter morning, Mr. Ray noticed Susie's jacket was too thin for the freezing temperatures. After his route, he quietly reached out to the school counselor, explaining the situation while respecting Susie's privacy. Within days, Susie received a warm winter coat through the school's assistance program—anonymously, just as Mr. Ray had hoped.

As the weeks passed, Susie's confidence grew. She began talking with other kids on the bus and even made a few friends. But Mr. Ray's impact didn't stop there. Inspired by his kindness, Susie signed up for the school's community service club, where she helped organize donations for other students in need—just like someone had done for her.

A Life Changed

Years later, at Elmwood High's graduation ceremony, Mr. Ray received an unexpected invitation. Onstage, Susie—now the valedictorian—shared her story: *"'There was a time when I felt invisible, like no one noticed or cared. But someone did. My school bus driver, Mr. Ray, saw me. He walked in my shoes, even when I didn't know how to ask for help. His kindness saved me from a very lonely path and showed me the power of caring for others."*

Mr. Ray wiped away tears as Susie received a standing ovation. He hadn't just driven a bus—he had driven a student toward a brighter future, proving that walking in someone else's shoes can lead them to places they never thought possible.

The role of a bus driver extends beyond just transporting students; it includes creating a positive, empathetic, and safe environment for them. Imagining what it would be like to live in your students' lives will help you find the compassion to treat them with kindness and gentleness. This approach not only supports the students' emotional and social development but also contributes to a more positive perception of the school system as a whole. Your insight underscores the need for empathy in all interactions with students, recognizing the various challenges they may face outside of school.

Reflection/Discussion Questions

- Why is it easy to forget the statistics on child hunger and abuse while carrying out our daily routines?

- What are some potential problems when helping students who have various needs?

- Can you remember a time when someone had empathy for you? Explain.

- Do you believe the statistics given in this chapter seem high or about right for your community? Why or why not?

15

The Best Bus Drivers Take Up for Students

Reflecting on being a student, many of us can vividly remember a time when someone within the school system stood up for us. Those moments often leave a lasting imprint, and the individuals involved—a teacher, coach, or even a bus driver—tend to hold a special place in our memories.

For instance, as a student-athlete, I deeply valued the moments when my coach would defend me against what we perceived as unfair calls. But not all my champions were on the sports field. I recall a time when a substitute teacher, who was filling in for my teacher Mrs. Porter, unfairly criticized me in front of my peers and my girlfriend. It was a humiliating experience that led me to skip this class for the two weeks Mrs. Porter was out, taking refuge in the gym instead.

Upon her return, Mrs. Porter immediately made it clear that the substitute would not be welcomed back to her classroom. Even when I confessed to my truancy, Mrs. Porter simply expressed understanding, never chastising me for my absence. Her support was so impactful that our bond endures to this day, with regular conversations that I cherish.

The bus driver on *The Simpsons* is a casually dressed daredevil named Otto. He is quick to come to the defense of Bart and the other students on his bus. So, despite his appearance, the students respect him. In fact, since the students think the school is anti-kids, and Otto is anti-school, he's on the kids' side. "The enemy of my enemy is my friend."

The recognition and appreciation didn't stop with the teachers. As athletes, my teammates and I were acutely aware of the school staff who supported us by attending our games. Their presence motivated us to excel in their classes and earned them our respect and protection against any student disrespect.

This sentiment extended to our bus drivers as well. Those who drove us to our games and then joined the stands, cheering us on, were not just drivers to us; they were supporters and part of the team. We could distinguish between those who genuinely cared and those who were there just for the paycheck.

Advocating for students when they have been wronged is a powerful method for building strong, positive relationships between educators and students. Research indicates that when teachers support students in challenging situations, it fosters trust and respect, leading to improved academic and social outcomes.[37] One study found that not only do positive teacher-student relationships improve the chances of that student performing well in school, but also that providing emotional support and standing up for students are key components of that relationship.[38] Another study reported that teachers who advocate for students and address injustices leads to decreased behavioral issues.[39] Combined, these two studies show that taking up for students can increase school performance and decrease acting out. While these studies looked at only teacher-student relationships, in my experience, *any* school employee can have these positive outcomes by showing students they have their backs. In the next section, I'll show how this can play out with bus drivers and their riders.

> **Have you ever had someone at the school level take up for you? What do you think about that person now?**

Vignettes

1. Defending Against Bullying

On a chilly morning, as students boarded the bus, Mrs. Bernard, the school bus driver, noticed a group of older students teasing a younger boy named Alex about his worn-out backpack. Recognizing the distress on Alex's face, Mrs. Bernard intervened by addressing the bullies firmly, stating that such behavior was unacceptable on her bus. She then had Alex sit up front, engaging him in a conversation about his interests, making him feel valued and safe. Over time, Alex began to look forward to his bus rides, knowing he had an ally in Mrs. Bernard. This intervention not only stopped the bullying but also built a trusting relationship between Alex and Mrs. Bernard.

2. Advocating in Disciplinary Misunderstandings

During an afternoon route, Ms. Garcia overheard a conversation among students about a classmate, Veronica, who had been accused of vandalizing a desk. Veronica explained her innocence to Ms. Garcia, expressing her frustration and fear of unjust punishment. Recognizing Veronica's distress and believing in her innocence, Ms. Garcia approached the school administration the next morning, sharing her observations and advocating for a fair review of the incident. Her intervention led to a reevaluation of the evidence, and Veronica was exonerated. Grateful for Ms. Garcia's support, Veronica developed a deep respect and trust for her, often seeking her advice during bus rides.

3. Supporting Against Unfair Academic Treatment

One afternoon, Mr. Davis noticed that Jordan, a cheerful student, was unusually quiet and appeared upset. Upon gentle inquiry, Jordan revealed that a teacher had publicly reprimanded him for not submitting an assignment, despite Jordan having turned it in on time. Feeling humiliated and unfairly treated, Jordan was reluctant to return to that class. Mr. Davis listened attentively and encouraged Jordan to discuss the matter with the teacher, offering to accompany him for support. The next day, Mr. Davis and Jordan met with the teacher, and it was discovered that the assignment had been misplaced. The teacher apologized to Jordan, and the situation was resolved. Jordan's appreciation for Mr. Davis's support strengthened their bond, and he felt more confident knowing he had an advocate in the school.

The lesson for all school employees, particularly those in roles like bus drivers and monitors, is that students are perceptive. They know who genuinely supports them and who is just going through the motions. It's the former who earns the students' respect and gratitude, both in the moment and in lasting memories.

Reflection/Discussion Questions

- Think about some of your favorite adults when you were in school. Did any of them ever take your side in an argument or take up for you? How did it make you feel? As an adult, have you ever had someone stand up for you? How did it make you feel?

- Have you ever taken up for a student? Did they appreciate it? Explain.

16

The Best Bus Drivers Know Students Are Always Watching Them

> " Children have never been very good at listening to their elders, but they have never failed to imitate them.[40]
> —James Baldwin, writer "

Have you ever been around very young children and said a cuss word? You immediately apologize because you know you just set a bad example for this young child. We all know how little children are always watching us and soaking up all types of information. They are always learning from their environment, making judgments about what is right and wrong from what they see and hear. Since 55 percent of communication is our body language, we need to know what signals we are emitting and what students are picking up subliminally.[41]

I remember that while interviewing students they would tell me about certain behaviors they noticed from bus drivers, teachers, etc. This included time off the clock, when they saw school staff in public. As a school administrator, it sometimes felt unfair that what I did in my free time could affect how kids and parents saw me as a school leader. But fair or not, they will make judgments. In my research, students noticed:

- if you spoke to them after school, at the grocery store, or elsewhere in the community.

- if you had beer in your cart at the supermarket.

- if you had children and whether or not they behaved well.

- how you treated every student and if you were fair or not.

- if you enjoyed your job or if you were just putting in your time.

- if you had school spirit and attended athletic and co-curricular events.

During our interviews with students, all of the above and more were mentioned to us by the students. The students would say things like, "The driver treats me fine but does not like certain students."

"What you do has far greater impact than what you say."[42] —Stephen R. Covey

As a teacher and coach, I was always surprised by how closely the students watched everything I did. I soon began to realize that I was basically onstage anytime I walked onto school property. Having this attitude can help you "get into character" when you start up your bus, creating an environment that sets you up to succeed.

Vignettes Illustrating the Importance of Mindful Behavior

The Grocery Store Encounter

Mr. Ramirez, a school bus driver, was off duty and shopping at a local grocery store. While waiting in line, he grew impatient and muttered a few complaints about the slow service. Unbeknownst to him, a student from his bus route, Janet, was in line behind him with her mother. The next day, Janet's mother mentioned the incident, expressing concern over the behavior Janet had witnessed. This encounter reminded Mr. Ramirez that his actions in public settings could influence his students, emphasizing the need for consistent positive behavior, even off the job.

The Weekend Sports Event

Ms. Eagan, a school bus driver, attended her son's soccer game one Saturday. During the match, she became visibly frustrated with the referee's calls, expressing her displeasure loudly. Several students from her bus route were present with their families and observed her reactions. The following week, a parent approached Ms. Eagan, noting that their child had mimicked similar outbursts during a school activity. This situation highlighted the importance of maintaining composure and demonstrating good sportsmanship, as students often emulate adult behaviors they observe outside the school environment.

The Community Fundraiser

Mrs. Allen, a school bus driver, volunteered at a community fundraiser over the weekend. She noticed several students from her bus route participating with their families. Throughout the event, Mrs. Allen displayed enthusiasm, cooperation, and a positive attitude. The following Monday, students excitedly shared their experiences from the fundraiser, mentioning how they saw Mrs. Allen helping out. This reinforced to Mrs. Allen that her positive actions in the community served as a role model for her students, demonstrating the value of community involvement and volunteerism.

To paraphrase Ralph Waldo Emerson, "what you *do* speaks so loudly about your character, I cannot hear what you *say*."[43] That is, people's judgment of your behavior far overshadows the weight of your words. Assume that if anything good or bad ever happens to you in the community, the kids will find out. As with all of us, if the students believe you like and care about them, they will give you the benefit of the doubt.[44] If they do not think you care about them, they can be quick to exploit your weaknesses. Always know the students are watching you . . . even when you think they are not.

My editor, Mike, shared a story about when he worked with middle school students in an after-school program. He and his coworker drove students from school to various places in the

136

community. One day, when their usual small bus was getting repaired, he had to drive one of the maintenance crew's vans instead. He picked up the students, they did their activities, and then got back in the van to be dropped off at the school for their parents to pick them up.

As he drove downhill into a flat stretch, a police car's lights came on behind him. He pulled over and realized how this must look. He was in a white van that belonged to someone he didn't know, packed with kids. All they needed to do was say one thing, even jokingly, and the cop would have arrested him. This was the moment of truth. Had he won them over? The police officer asked for license and registration, which he was able to find and provide. The officer looked in back, proceeded to explain that the speed limit went from thirty-five to twenty-five at the bottom of the hill and he'd been going too fast. The officer gave him a warning, investigated the back seat again, then walked back to his cruiser. Mike let out a big exhale, thankful that the kids could grasp the weight of the situation and did not have an axe to grind. They quietly drove the last few blocks to the school for drop-off.

At this point, the kids had already texted their parents, some of whom had driven by the van as it was pulled over, so they all knew what had happened as the van pulled up to the school. Again, Mike was nervous that the parents were going to let him have it for getting pulled over while driving their kids. As he got out and the children piled out of the van, the parents all burst out in laughter. "They got you, too, huh?" one of them said. Apparently, this was a well-known speed trap in town, and everybody around there knew to slow down as a police car was often waiting to pull over unsuspecting drivers. One of them gave him a pat on the back as if to say, "You're one of us now." Mike let out a sigh of relief and even joined in the laughter, thankful that he'd been given the benefit of the doubt by the parents who trusted him with their kids.

Reflection/Discussion Questions

- List several locations outside of school where you might see some of your student riders. Do you view this as a time to strengthen the relationship?

- What are some ways to leave a good or bad impression of yourself with a student rider without communicating directly with the student rider?

- Are some students watching to make sure you follow all the transportation rules while driving the bus? What might be their thoughts if they see you break a rule? Have you formed opinions about your boss based on what you have seen or heard when they are off work? Explain.

17

The Best Bus Drivers Don't Do Dumb Things

> **"** It takes twenty years to build a reputation and five minutes to ruin it. If you think about that, you'll do things differently.[45]
> —Warren Buffett, philanthropist **"**

I have written several articles about the impact of doing dumb things, mostly in the context of the public school setting. My primary interest in this topic stems from the fact that I believe we can recover from almost any mistake we make when providing services to others, with just one exception. Recovery is very hard and sometimes impossible when we do dumb things. For my purposes, the definition of a dumb thing is when our mistake lacks *common sense* or is so erroneous that it may cause mental or physical harm to the customer. One litmus test to decide if an error is a simple mistake or one of the "dumb things" I'm referring to is if a young child could be given all the necessary facts and not make the same mistake. Even kids can grasp common sense.

Billy the bus driver had been a well-loved resident in his town for over two decades. His dedication went beyond just safely delivering children to and from school. He knew every kid by name, every parent by face, and was always the first to volunteer when the school needed extra help. If a child forgot their lunch at home, Billy would stop by the house and pick it up. If someone was struggling, Billy was the one they could count on. The small town trusted him with their most precious cargo, and Billy never let them down.

When Billy's fiftieth birthday rolled around, the community decided to surprise him with a celebration at the local bar. It was an evening full of laughter, stories, and a deep sense of appreciation for the man who had done so much for the town. For once, Billy allowed himself to relax. He bought a round of drinks for the group as a gesture of his usual generosity, unaware that one of the recipients was a seventeen-year-old girl who had been on his bus just that morning.

As the evening wore on, friends offered to drive Billy home, but Billy, stubborn in his independence, insisted he was fine. On his way home, another car ran a red light and collided with Billy's vehicle. Thankfully, nobody was hurt. Although the accident wasn't his fault, the officer on the scene administered a breathalyzer test, which revealed Billy had been drinking. He was charged with a DUI. News spread quickly through the small town, and headlines in the local paper made matters worse: "Beloved School Bus Driver Arrested for DUI and Serving Alcohol to a Minor."

The girl's mother, furious and protective, pressed charges against Billy for buying alcohol for her underage daughter. Though the charges were later dropped, and his DUI reduced to a lesser offense, the damage was done. Billy's once-sterling reputation had been irreparably tarnished. The town's trust, carefully built over twenty years of selfless service, crumbled in an instant.

Billy's story is a somber reminder of how a few misguided decisions can unravel years of goodwill. Despite his remorse and the legal resolutions, Billy could not recover the trust and admiration he had worked so hard to earn. He had become the cautionary tale of the town—a reminder that even the best among us can falter, and that some mistakes, though not malicious, can have consequences that linger far longer than the moment they were made.

Examples of dumb things by bus drivers I have witnessed that make a recovery difficult include:

1. Operating with an "I am the boss mentality, and I do not answer to anyone else" mindset
2. Using all types of slurs and inappropriate language
3. Being an unsafe driver
4. Being a terrible adult to other bus drivers and monitors
5. Breaking laws in the community

An Unexpected Trip to the Amusement Park

I like to tell this story of a bus driver who failed to use common sense because it is so outrageous. In a bizarre mix-up, a bus driver picked up a group of thirty middle school students, and instead of bringing them to school, where they were supposed to go, she brought them to Six Flags Great Adventures theme park, miles down the highway.

The children on board were shocked and scared to see the bus driver going out of town and they asked her to stop, telling her that they were supposed to go to school and not on a field trip. Then the children pleaded for her to call the school and double-check. But the bus driver did not listen. At this point, some of the children feared they were being abducted.

Without a single adult on board other than the driver, the students took matters into their own hands, calling their parents and the school to inform them of what was happening. One child had the principal on her cell phone and tried to give the phone to the driver. The driver told her she was not allowed to handle the cell phone while she was driving the bus. Eventually, law enforcement caught up to the bus and stopped it from going to the theme park. An officer boarded the bus to inform the bus driver to go back to the school and stayed aboard the bus to ensure they got back safely.

What was going through this bus driver's head, I'll never know. Common sense would say that if this many kids were sure she was making a mistake, maybe she should at least double-check. Why on earth would a group of middle-schoolers plead for the bus driver to take them to school instead of to Six Flags? Shouldn't they be ecstatic at the amazing surprise field trip? It doesn't add up at all. The bus driver refusing to listen to anyone, including adults on the phone, is a perfect example of not using common sense and doing a very, very dumb thing that could have cost her her job.

It's important to note that doing "dumb things" makes recovery almost impossible. I have stories of bus drivers being intoxicated while driving, and some of them wrecked the bus with students on board. I have other stories of bus drivers sleeping with underage students, being involved with child pornography, and several others who committed federal offenses. Sure, even the best bus drivers will make mistakes, but they're honest mistakes and ones from which they can recover. But doing dumb things often leads to drivers losing their jobs and even their careers, all while making their schools look bad from the publicity they draw.

Reflection/Discussion Questions

- Why are dumb mistakes so hard to recover from?

- As a customer, what are some dumb things that have been done to you?

- As an employee, what are some dumb things that you have done in your current job or other jobs?

18

The Best Bus Drivers Enjoy Their Jobs

> " Pleasure in the job puts perfection in the work.[46]
> —Aristotle, philosopher "

The enjoyment a bus driver experiences in their work is palpable and can profoundly affect the atmosphere on the bus, much like how the enthusiasm of any professional in a customer service role influences customer satisfaction. When school bus drivers enjoy their jobs, it becomes evident in their interactions with students and their approaches to their daily routes.

A bus driver who takes pleasure in their responsibilities often greets each student with a smile, remembers their names, and engages in friendly conversations. This positive demeanor sets a welcoming tone for the day, helping students start their mornings with optimism and end their day with a sense of calm. Drivers who enjoy their jobs are typically more patient and understanding, which is crucial when dealing with the dynamic and sometimes challenging behavior of young students. Drivers' genuine care and attention can help manage and mitigate on-bus conflicts more effectively, maintaining a safe and harmonious environment for all.

Moreover, a bus driver's job satisfaction is closely linked to the quality of the service they provide. Just as in any customer service industry, the level of commitment and enthusiasm of the service provider can dramatically enhance the customer's experience. In the case of school transportation, the "customers" are the students and their parents, who entrust the driver with the safety and well-being of their children. When bus drivers are passionate about their roles, they're more likely to be diligent, proactive about safety, and dedicated to their duty, giving parents peace of mind and fostering trust within the school community.

The Transformation of Mr. Morrissey

For years, Mr. Morrissey had been the kind of school bus driver that students dreaded. He wasn't mean, exactly, just perpetually grumpy. He often sighed heavily, rolled his eyes at loud kids, and occasionally muttered under his breath about how he "couldn't wait to retire in five years."

"Kids these days," he would grumble. "No respect, no manners."

He wasn't entirely wrong. Some students were disrespectful, others messy, and a few never seemed to sit down, no matter how many times he told them to. But what Mr. Morrissey didn't realize was that his attitude only made things worse. The kids mirrored his energy—if he was short-tempered and cold, they became unruly and indifferent. Then, one winter morning, an encounter changed everything.

Mr. Morrissey had picked up some groceries for dinner. When he reached the checkout, instead of the usual moody, uninspired greeting he was used to getting, the cashier greeted him with a bright smile.

"Hi there! How's your day going?" she asked cheerfully.

Mr. Morrissey blinked, startled by the warmth in her voice. "Oh, you know . . . another day," he said.

"Well, I hope it turns out to be a great one!" she replied as she handed him his receipt. As he walked to his car, he realized something—his mood had changed. It seemed like she actually *enjoyed* her job, and that positivity rolled over to him. He thought, *If that was true for me, is it also true for the kids on my bus?*

The next morning, Mr. Morrissey decided to try something different. Instead of scowling as the first group of students climbed aboard, he greeted them with a smile.

"Good morning, everyone!" he said in a tone far friendlier than usual.

The students hesitated for a moment, exchanging puzzled glances. But then one brave soul responded.

"Uh . . . good morning, Mr. Morrissey?"

He nodded. Progress.

As the days passed, he started injecting a little fun into his job. He played upbeat music at a low volume during the rides. He told corny jokes over the speaker.

"What kind of bagel flies?" he asked one morning.

Silence. Then, from the back of the bus, a voice called out, "I don't know—what?"

"A plain bagel!" he announced, grinning.

Groans and laughter filled the bus.

Then, something incredible started happening. Not only was he starting to, dare I say, enjoy his job, but the once rowdy kids had become more respectful as well. They greeted him with smiles, fewer arguments broke out, and even the students who used to cause trouble seemed to relax. The bus no longer felt like a prison on wheels—it felt like a community.

One day, a student named Jamie, who had always been shy, stopped before getting off the bus.

"Mr. Morrissey?" she said quietly.

"Yeah, kiddo?"

"I just wanted to say . . . I like riding your bus now. It's fun."

Mr. Morrissey felt a lump rise in his throat. He nodded. "That means a lot, Jamie. Thanks for telling me."

Over time, Mr. Morrissey realized he didn't have to hate his job. Sure, retirement was still on the horizon, but for the first time in years, he wasn't counting down the days. In fact, the more he radiated positivity while driving with the students, the more he enjoyed his work. It was not just a means to an end anymore.

Mr. Morrissey had discovered something important—his attitude didn't just affect him. It affected every student who stepped onto his bus. And when he chose to be positive, the whole ride became better for everyone.

As he pulled up to the school one morning, he saw his reflection in the rearview mirror. The old, grumpy bus driver was gone. In its place was a man who had learned that happiness, like laughter and kindness, is contagious.

> "People rarely succeed unless they have fun in what they are doing."[47] —Dale Carnegie

The ripple effects of a bus driver's job satisfaction can also impact the broader school culture. Drivers who are enthusiastic about their work often go beyond the call of duty, participating in school events, supporting students in their extracurricular activities, and becoming a valued part of the school community. Their positive attitude can inspire and motivate students, contribute to a supportive and engaging school experience, and enhance student retention and satisfaction.

The Power of a Positive Attitude

The positive attitude of school bus drivers is an essential component in the educational experience of students and the wider school community. Research has shown that the attitude of service providers can spread and profoundly affect those around them.[48] Just as a customer service representative's demeanor can make or break a customer's perception of a brand, a bus driver's attitude can significantly influence a student's and their family's perception of the school.

School bus drivers are often the first point of contact for students each day; their warm greetings, optimism, and friendliness can set a positive tone for the students' entire day.

Southwest Airlines hiring philosophy: We hire for attitude and train for skills.

Moreover, bus drivers are in a unique position to observe and interact with students outside the formal classroom setting. They can build trust and rapport, which can be especially important for students who may face challenges in other areas of their lives. When bus drivers show that they care, they become another positive adult figure in students' lives, contributing to a supportive educational environment. This positive culture not only benefits students but also enhances job satisfaction among drivers, creating a virtuous cycle of happiness that benefits the entire school ecosystem.

In the context of communication with parents, a bus driver's positive attitude is equally critical. Parents trust bus drivers to transport their children safely, and drivers who communicate effectively and warmly can reassure parents that their children are in good hands. A positive encounter with the bus driver can also alleviate any concerns parents might have about their child's day at school.

Furthermore, in situations where bus drivers face challenges or conflicts, either with students or parents, a positive attitude is key to de-escalation. By maintaining composure and a helpful disposition, bus drivers can navigate these situations more effectively, preventing them from escalating and ensuring that all parties feel heard and respected.

In essence, when school bus drivers genuinely enjoy their jobs, it's reflected in the quality of their interactions, the safety of their driving, and the overall satisfaction of students and parents. Their role is not just to drive, it's to be a positive starting and ending point to each student's school day, to support the educational mission, and to contribute to the creation of a positive community. The joy they derive from their work is infectious, fostering a more pleasant and effective educational environment for everyone.

Reflection/Discussion Questions

- Would you rather do business with a company where the employees enjoy their jobs? Why or why not?

- When interviewing, what are some thoughts on hiring transportation employees with a great attitude?

- When you go to a restaurant, do you expect employees of the restaurant to have a good attitude? Might your opinion of the restaurant be based on the attitude of your server?

- Can a great attitude or a bad attitude of one employee make or ruin your entire dining experience? Explain.

19

The Best Bus Drivers Keep Backstage Issues Backstage

> " The show must go on—and no one needs to see the chaos behind the curtain.
> —Unknown "

I was at the counter of a fast-food restaurant where two employees were arguing and cussing at each other. I immediately lost my appetite and walked out. Have you ever had a waiter or waitress confess their horrible life story to you? Perhaps they break down and cry. Maybe they talk about their mean boss or even put down the place where you are about to eat. Does this help you enjoy your meal? Do you feel any better about the restaurant? I can only assume the waiter or waitress thinks you might feel sorry for her and give a large tip.

I was a central office employee in a school district and received a call from a parent that a fight had broken out in the high school cafeteria. The parent asked about the knives that were involved. I told the parent that if there were knives involved, I would have already heard about it. She told me she has a friend who works in the school cafeteria, and thus she believed this had occurred. Then she went so far as to ask me to not try to cover it up. The comment bothered me, but I let it go as her information could have been correct.

I promised the parent that I would get to the bottom of it and get back to her. In school administration, you just know when you have to stop what you are doing and take care of the immediate problem. This was one of those times.

I called the school principal, district food service director, and high school cafeteria manager into my office. I wanted to know how the fight in the cafeteria was handled, down to the last detail. All three looked at me as if I had three heads and said there was a little pushing that occurred, but it did not even rise to the level of a fight. Besides that, there was no other violence in any of the cafeterias on this day. I then asked about utensils used on this day in the cafeteria—specifically about knives. They responded that only plastic sporks had been used. I told them to interview each cook and find out how this parent could have been told about knives being used.

It turned out, one of the cafeteria monitors told her friend who was a cook at the middle school that she was afraid to break up the fight because, who knows, the student could have been carrying a knife.

I called the parent back and enjoyed telling her that her info came from someone not even in their child's school. She even admitted that she might not have heard the knife story as she had portrayed it to me. I then had to say, "You mean you accused me of covering up a story that you made up?" We laughed together and she thanked me for doing the investigation. She also said she just wants the school to be safe. I thanked her for calling me and giving me a chance to correct the narrative.

It was yet another chance for me to remind our leaders to urge their staff to keep backstage issues backstage. All it takes is for one rumor, especially by a school employee, to hit social media and now we have a major public relations problem. My hope is that all school employees understand that we now have competition, and all employees are positive public relations agents for the school district.

Knowing how to keep backstage issues backstage is especially important for public school bus drivers who hear all kinds of true and untrue things that go on in a school district. Public schools are where many rumors and conspiracy theories thrive each and every day.

In an environment where school choice is increasingly prevalent, and parents have the option to send their children to charter schools or homeschool, the reputation of public schools becomes even more significant. Here's why maintaining confidentiality and professionalism is vital for bus drivers and bus monitors:

- **Impact on School Reputation:** Rumors, whether true or false, can significantly impact the reputation of a school district. Bus drivers are often seen as extensions of the school community, and their words can carry weight. Spreading negative information can lead to a loss of trust and confidence in the school system.

- **Influence on Student Choices:** In an age where parents and students have more educational options, the choice of school can be influenced by the perceived environment and culture of the school. Negative information, especially if it spreads unchecked, can sway decisions, potentially leading to a decrease in enrollment in public schools.

- **Role as Trusted Adults:** Bus drivers are not just transport providers; they often hold a position of trust and influence with students. It's crucial that they use this position responsibly, fostering a positive and supportive environment rather than contributing to the spread of rumors.

- **Professionalism and Ethical Responsibility:** As with any profession, there's an ethical responsibility to maintain confidentiality and professionalism. Discussing rumors or sensitive information with students or parents is not only unprofessional but could also lead to misinformation and unwarranted concerns.

- **Job Security:** In this competitive educational environment, the actions of all staff members, including bus drivers, can impact the overall performance and standing of a school district. Engaging in gossip or spreading rumors can lead to disciplinary action or even job loss, as it undermines the mission and values of the educational institution.

- **Correcting Misinformation:** If bus drivers or monitors are concerned about a rumor or story they've heard, the appropriate course of action would be to discuss it privately with their immediate supervisor. This allows for any issues to be addressed internally and professionally, avoiding unnecessary escalation.

A Professional Does Not Spread Gossip

In the small town of Brookfield, everyone knew each other, and news traveled fast—sometimes too fast. Liz Wilson, a longtime school bus driver for Brookfield Unified, was well-liked for her friendly demeanor and easy conversation. She enjoyed chatting with parents and neighbors during her breaks at the local diner, sharing stories about her daily bus routes. But sometimes, Liz shared more than she should have.

A Habit of Oversharing

It started innocently enough—funny stories about kids forgetting their lunch boxes or getting their backpacks stuck in the bus door. But over time, Liz's stories drifted into more sensitive territory: "Did you hear the Smith kid got in trouble again? That family's always causing problems."

"Mrs. Carson from the transportation office messed up the bus schedules *again*. No wonder we're always running late."

Liz didn't see the harm. After all, it was just harmless venting among familiar faces—or so she thought.

The Rumor Mill Turns

One Friday afternoon, Liz was chatting at the diner when she mentioned something she overheard from a school staff meeting: that budget cuts might affect special education transportation. She framed it as gossip, assuming it wouldn't go far.

But in a tight-knit community like Brookfield, that was a mistake. Within hours, concerned parents were calling the school district office, demanding answers. The district was blindsided—the budget discussions weren't final, and no decisions had been made.

To make matters worse, the Smith family found out what Liz had been saying about their son. They filed a formal complaint with the school board, citing unprofessional conduct and a breach of privacy.

Facing the Consequences

By Monday, Liz was called into a meeting with the transportation supervisor and the district superintendent. Her oversharing had caused a community-wide stir, creating mistrust between the district and families. Worse, it violated the district's confidentiality policy.

Though Liz kept her job, she was formally reprimanded and required to attend professional conduct training. Her relationships with some parents and coworkers never fully recovered. Trust once broken is hard to rebuild.

A Lesson Learned

Humbled, Liz took the experience as a wake-up call. She realized that her job wasn't just driving a bus—it was representing the school district every time she interacted with the community. She learned that keeping "backstage" matters private wasn't about hiding the truth—it was about respecting boundaries and maintaining trust.

From then on, Liz kept her conversations focused on safe topics like weather, sports, and local events. Her stories about the bus route became lighthearted tales of acts of kindness and funny mix-ups—but never at the expense of anyone's reputation or privacy.

Liz's experience taught the entire Brookfield community a powerful lesson: even small-town talk can cause big-time problems. Keeping "backstage issues backstage" isn't just good policy—it's the foundation of trust, respect, and professionalism.

In summary, in the current educational climate, where the competition for student enrollment is high, the role of school bus drivers extends beyond transportation. Their conduct, discretion, and professionalism play a crucial role in shaping the perception and reputation of public schools. It's essential for them to be aware of the impact of their actions and words and to adhere to a standard of professionalism that supports the integrity of the educational system.

Reflection/Discussion Questions

- As an employee in a school district, what behaviors should be kept backstage?

- What are some items or actions that companies should try to keep backstage? Why is it more important than ever for all school district employees to be positive public relations agents?

20

The Best Bus Drivers Are Professionals

> " Being a professional is doing the things you love to do on the days you don't feel like doing them.[49]
> —Julius Erving, former basketball player "

The best bus drivers have a professional appearance and attitude. Research states that we form opinions of people in the first seven seconds of meeting them.[50] We also know that it takes a lot of extra work to change a first impression.[51] By knowing these two facts about human behavior, we can get off to a great start with students by looking and acting like a professional. Why not start off putting your best foot forward?

Many bus drivers I've known didn't realize just how much they mattered to their schools and communities. The safety and well-being of your riders is majorly important, and bus drivers need to be trusted with their precious cargo. You regularly make split-second decisions to avoid crashes, drive in inclement weather, and stay focused on the road with about seventy distractions behind you. By putting your best foot forward— looking and acting like a professional—you're demonstrating that not only can you do your job well, but you understand that there's more to the job and to earning the trust of your school and its families.

The Professional Appearance

A study involving undergraduate students and their professors revealed that formal attire worn by instructors may have a positive effect on student attendance and performance.[52] As an educator, I always felt the students behaved and performed better in my classes when I dressed up. I experienced this feeling for about eight years when I was teaching high school students. During these years, I also coached two sports and taught a weight lifting class. I always dressed up when teaching my other classes and would dress down to lift weights with the students. Depending on the time weight lifting was offered, I might have a few classes right before or right after the weight lifting class. Originally, I wore my weight lifting clothes in my regular classroom to keep from having to change clothes. I noticed immediately the students did not take me as seriously in the classroom when wearing my weight lifting attire. Even though it was a lot of trouble, I changed clothes as many as three times a day because I found it made me a more effective teacher. At the time, I didn't know any of the research. I just knew what worked best with my high school students.

The Transformation of Mr. Jim

Mr. Jim had been a school bus driver for nearly fifteen years. He loved the kids and took pride in getting them to and from school safely. But deep down, he never thought of himself as anything more than just a driver. He wore jeans and a T-shirt most days, and he didn't think much about his appearance. His job was to drive the bus—nothing more.

One chilly February morning, Jim received the heartbreaking news that his longtime friend Larry had passed away. That evening, Jim dressed in his best suit and tie to attend the visitation. As he drove to the funeral home, he felt different—more composed, more confident.

On his way home, he decided to stop by the local car dealership to check on a truck he'd been eyeing for months. The moment he stepped through the door, a salesman rushed to greet him.

"Good evening, sir! How can I assist you today?" The salesman's enthusiasm caught Jim off guard. Normally, he'd have to wander around the lot before anyone acknowledged him.

"Just looking," Jim said hesitantly.

"Of course! Let me know if you have any questions. We take care of our customers!" the salesman beamed.

Jim nodded and walked around, noticing how attentive the staff was. No one dismissed him or ignored him as they had in the past.

Next, he stopped at a clothing store to return a dress his wife had bought online. The moment he stepped inside, a sales clerk greeted him warmly.

"Welcome, sir! What can I help you with today?" she asked with a bright smile.

"Just returning this," Jim replied, holding up the bag.

"Of course! But, might I interest you in some of our newest arrivals? We have some wonderful suits that would look great on you."

Jim chuckled and shook his head. "No, just the return today."

As he drove home, he couldn't shake the feeling that something was different. Why had people treated him so well today? Then, as he walked into the kitchen and shared his experience with his wife, she laughed knowingly.

"Jim, don't you see? It's how you're dressed. People see you differently when you look professional."

Jim sat back in his chair, stunned. He thought about the people he respected—his doctor, his dentist, police officers. They all dressed in a way that commanded respect. He had never thought about it before, but it all made sense.

That night, Jim made a decision. He was going to change the way he saw himself. The next morning, instead of his usual jeans and T-shirt, he put on a collared shirt, a nice pair of slacks, and shined his shoes. As he stepped onto the bus, the students noticed immediately.

"Whoa, Mr. Jim! Got a hot date?" one of the kids teased.

"Nah, just decided it was time to look like the professional I am," Jim replied with a grin.

Over the next few weeks, something incredible happened. The students started treating him with more respect. Discipline issues decreased. He found that when he dressed as a professional, the kids responded in kind. He no longer felt like "just a bus driver"—he felt like an important part of their daily lives.

By the end of the school year, Jim was known as one of the most beloved bus drivers in the district. Parents requested him, students listened to him, and he found more joy in his job than ever before.

He thought back to Larry and smiled. His friend's passing had given him a wonderful gift: a new perspective. From that day forward, Jim changed his thinking about only dressing up for special occasions. He dressed as the professional he was, every single day.

This narrative underscores a fundamental truth: in roles of authority—especially those involving impressionable individuals like students—personal appearance and hygiene significantly influence how one is perceived and treated. Looking like a professional fosters respect and order, while a more casual or unkempt appearance can lead to disrespect and chaos. Maintaining a neat and clean appearance is not merely about personal pride but also about setting a standard and creating an environment conducive to respect and discipline.

Presenting yourself as a polished professional demonstrates your dedication to your job and respect for the students, parents, and school district. Being clean and well-dressed builds trust and sets the right example. It shows you care, and that you understand the significance of your role in shaping first impressions of the school system.

Remember, professionalism isn't just about how others perceive you—it's a reflection of how seriously you take your job. When you look the part, that inspires confidence in everyone who entrusts you with their children.

Act Professionally by Being Consistent in Mood and Behavior

Have you ever been around someone moody? Or had to guess what version of that person you were meeting that day and then had to adjust your behavior accordingly? One day they excitedly talk with you about the weekend or show you pictures of their children or grandchildren, then the next day they do not even speak to you. Or worse, maybe they snap at you or complain about their bad day. When we encounter people whose moods are unpredictable, it can be hard to trust them or feel comfortable when interacting with them.

Students are no different. They like and expect us to be consistent each day without having to guess about our mood. While interviewing students for my previous book, I heard stories about adults losing their tempers and students making fun of adults who broke down and started crying.[53] While some students showed empathy for adults who cried as they became frustrated with student behavior, in our research, I never found any student who *respected* such adults or their behavior.

Occasionally during a speaking engagement, I am asked if it is okay for adults to just have a bad day. I can tell my audience is somewhat surprised when I say no. Do I expect the surgeon who is operating on me to have a bad day? Do I expect the young man at the McDonald's drive-through to be rude to me because his girlfriend just broke up with him? Might I tell the manager or give him a bad review? I believe we are all professionals, and students and parents should see us that way. We need to *compartmentalize* any issues in our own lives—that is a key aspect of being a professional. The best bus drivers maintain consistency each day and with every student and adult interaction.

Being Consistent Is Professional

A consistent, positive demeanor from a driver can shape students' bus experiences, reinforcing feelings of safety, respect, and belonging. Here are ways school bus drivers can demonstrate consistent behavior beyond routines and procedures.

1. Consistent Tone and Demeanor

A school bus driver should maintain a calm, respectful, and approachable tone, regardless of the situation. For example, if students are loud or restless, the driver addresses the situation with a steady, firm, yet polite tone instead of shouting or showing frustration. This consistency builds trust and ensures students know how the driver will respond in both calm and challenging situations.

2. Predictable Emotional Responses

Students feel safer when they know what emotional response to expect from the driver. Emotional stability can defuse tense situations. When students argue or act out, a driver who consistently listens before responding helps students feel heard while reinforcing fairness. Students are less likely to escalate conflicts when they trust the driver's measured response.

3. Positive Greetings and Farewells

Small gestures repeated daily create a foundation of reliability. A simple, consistent greeting or goodbye can shape how students view their bus ride. The driver makes a habit of greeting every student with a smile or a friendly "Good morning!" and saying, "Have a great day!" when they leave. Even on tough days, maintaining this positive behavior helps set a supportive tone.

Consistency in behavior helps school bus drivers create a supportive, predictable, and safe environment for students. When drivers maintain steady emotional responses, they become the trusted, respected professionals students want in their daily lives. This relational consistency builds a positive school culture from the moment students step on the bus.

If you look and act like a professional, students *will* behave better on your bus. They will respect your rules and listen to your directions. I 100 percent believe this, as I've seen it countless times in public education in all different departments. Being a professional doesn't take a lot of work, money, or time, and the impact is well worth it. Not only will it make your job easier, but you will also get the satisfaction of knowing you are being a professional. That, in turn, may even create job security for you.

Reflection/Discussion Questions

- Do you enjoy being around friends or family who are not consistent in their interactions with you?

- Can you imagine working for a supervisor that treated you differently each day?

- While boarding a plane, the captain greets you, but instead of their professional suit, they have on old, worn-out jeans and a dirty T-shirt. Might you lose a little confidence in the flight? Why or why not?

- Do you have certain expectations of dress when you visit your doctor? What are some other occupations where you have similar expectations of dress?

- Have you ever been treated differently based on how you were dressed?

- What are some characteristics that make someone seem professional? Unprofessional?

- Should a bus driver be considered a professional?

Supplemental Material

🚌 School Bus Driver Student Survey

We want to make sure your ride to and from school is safe, respectful, and positive. Please take a few minutes to answer these questions about your school bus driver. Your feedback helps us improve!

1. Does your bus driver greet you or say something friendly when you get on or off the bus?

- Always
- Most of the time
- Sometimes
- Never

2. Does your bus driver know your name?

- Yes
- No
- I'm not sure

3. Does your driver try to get to know students (like asking how your day was or talking about your interests)?

- Yes, often
- Sometimes
- Rarely
- Never

4. Has your driver ever contacted your parent/guardian for any reason?

- Yes
- I think so
- No
- I'm not sure

5. Does your driver treat all students with respect?

- Always
- Most of the time
- Sometimes
- Rarely

6. Do you feel safe while riding the bus?

- Yes, always
- Most of the time
- Sometimes
- No

7. If there is a problem on the bus, does your driver handle it fairly and respectfully?

- Yes
- Sometimes
- Not really
- I'm not sure

8. Do you think your bus driver cares about the students on their bus?

- Yes
- A little
- Not really
- No

9. What's one thing your bus driver does really well?
(Open-ended response)

_____

_____

_____

10. Is there anything you think your driver could do better?
(Open-ended response)

_____

_____

_____

Connect Four

This year our district is making connecting with students a focus. Our transportation department is going to use the slogan "Connect Four" as we try to connect with four students each month. Document your information on the cards provided until you have information on all your riders.

Month _____

Rider _____

Nickname _____

Age _____

Birthdate _____

School _____

Activities _____

Hobbies _____

Favorite Subject _____

Favorite Teacher _____

Future Goals _____

Family Members _____

Anything Else? _____

Other Books by Kelly E. Middleton

www.kellymiddleton.com

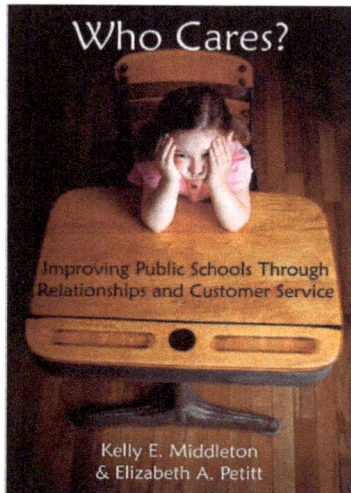

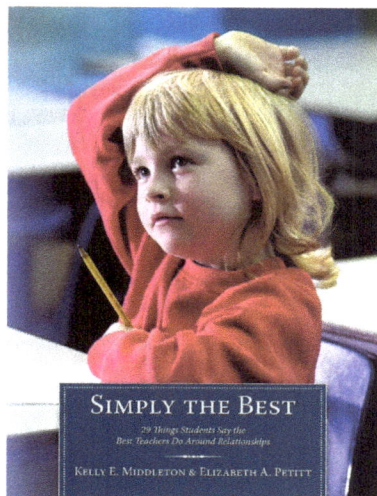

Who Cares?
Improving Public Schools Through Relationships and Customer Service
Kelly E. Middleton & Elizabeth A. Petitt

SIMPLY THE BEST
29 Things Students Say the Best Teachers Do Around Relationships
KELLY E. MIDDLETON & ELIZABETH A. PETITT

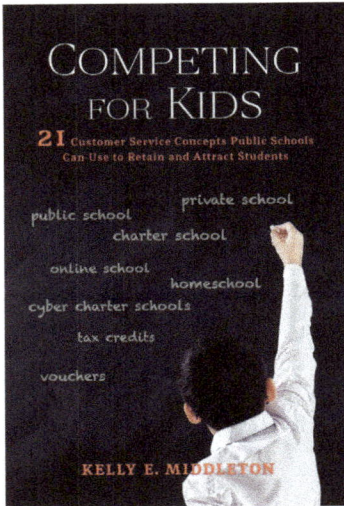

COMPETING
FOR KIDS
21 Customer Service Concepts Public Schools
Can Use to Retain and Attract Students

private school

public school

charter school

online school

homeschool

cyber charter schools

tax credits

vouchers

KELLY E. MIDDLETON

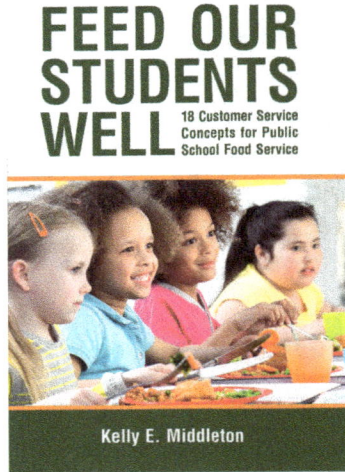

FEED OUR
STUDENTS
WELL 18 Customer Service
Concepts for Public
School Food Service

Kelly E. Middleton

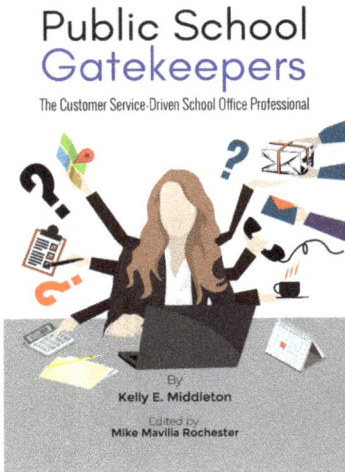

Public School
Gatekeepers
The Customer Service-Driven School Office Professional

By
Kelly E. Middleton
Edited by
Mike Mavilia Rochester

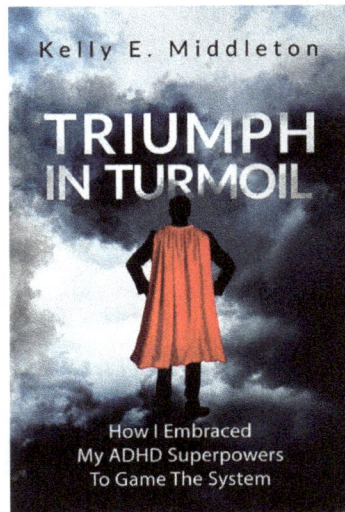

Kelly E. Middleton

TRIUMPH
IN TURMOIL

How I Embraced
My ADHD Superpowers
To Game The System

Works Cited

1   Thaler, Mike. *The School Bus Driver from the Black Lagoon*. New York: Scholastic, 1999. Print.

2   Middleton, Kelly, and Petitt, Elizabeth A. *Who Cares? Improving Public Schools Through Relationships and Customer Service*. Tucson, Arizona: Wheatmark, 2007. Print.

3   Isidore, Chris. "GM Was America's Largest Automaker for Nearly a Century. It Was Just Dethroned by Toyota." CNN Business. January, 4, 2022. Web. Accessed May 17. 2025. https://www.cnn.com/2022/01/04/business/toyota-gm-us-auto-sales-leader/index.html.

4   Farnham Street Media Inc. "Who Is Richard Feynman? The Curious Character Who Mastered Thinking and Physics." *fs.blog*. Web. Accessed May 17, 2025. https://fs.blog/intellectual-giants/richard-feynman/#:~:text=Richard%20Feynman%20Quotes,what%20they%20call%20the%20bird%E2%80%A6.

5   Kirby, Stephanie. "50 Going Above and Beyond Quotes About Doing More Than You Have To." *Everyday Power*. September 27, 2023. Web. Accessed May 17, 2025. https://everydaypower.com/going-above-and-beyond-quotes/.

6   Denove, Chris, and Power IV, James D. *Satisfaction: How Every Great Company Listens to the Voice of the Customer.* New York: Penguin Group, 2006. Print.

7   Kelly, Brenna R. "Like a Grandfather for Every Student." *Kentucky Teacher*, September 2016. Web. Accessed May 17, 2025. https://www.kentuckyteacher.org/features/2016/09/like-a-grandfather-for-every-student/.

8   Sanborn, Mark. *The Fred Factor: How Passion in Your Work and Life Can Turn the Ordinary into the Extraordinary.* New York: Currency Doubleday, 2004. Print.

9   Sicard, Crystal. "Carlisle County School Bus Driver Receives 2023 Fred Award for Acts of Kindness, Making 'the World a Better Place.'" *Kentucky Teacher*, August 14, 2023. Web. Accessed May 17, 2025. https://www.kentuckyteacher.org/features/2023/08/carlisle-county-school-bus-driver-receives-2023-fred-award-for-acts-of-kindness-making-the-world-a-better-place/.

10   Arif, Saba. "Practicing Happiness to Boost Your Success." *Medium*, August 31, 2017. Web. Accessed May 17, 2025. https://medium.com/@sabaarif09.sa/there-is-a-very-famous-saying-of-mother-teresa-peace-begins-with-a-smile-e3ba3b60246c.

11   Mehrabian, Albert. *Silent Messages: Implicit Communication of Emotions and Attitudes.* New York: Wadsworth Publishing. Co., 1980. Print.

12   Siegel, Emily. "Why Phil Rosenthal Starves Himself Before Filming Episodes of 'Somebody Feed Phil.'" *Forbes*. July

5, 2018. Accessed July 7, 2025. https://www.forbes.com/sites/emilysiegel/2018/07/05/somebody-feed-phil-phil-rosenthal/.

13   Middleton, Kelly, and Petitt, Elizabeth A. *Simply the Best: 29 Things Students Say the Best Teachers Do Around Relationships*. Bloomington, Indiana: AuthorHouse, 2010. Print.

14   Mitchell, Margaret. *Gone with the Wind*. New York: Macmillan, 1936. Print.

15   Ginis, Abbie. "Quick Ways to Build Rapport with Students." *Swing Education*, September 13, 2024. Web. Accessed June 12, 2025. https://swingeducation.com/sub-success-resource-center/quick-ways-to-build-rapport-with-students/#:~:text=Have%20a%20sense%20of%20humor,students%20have%20a%20better%20experience.

16   "Aguidon Quotes." Goodreads. Web. Accessed May 17, 2025. https://www.goodreads.com/quotes/7332060-sometimes-one-needs-another-pair-of-eyes-to-see-things.

17   Kizer, Jennifer Graham. "Bus Driver's Act of Kindness Saves the Day for Child Who Forgot It Was Pajama Day." Ksby.com, February 16, 2024. Web. Accessed June 13, 2025. https://www.ksby.com/bus-drivers-act-of-kindness-saves-the-day-for-child-who-forgot-it-was-pajama-day.

18   Carnegie, Dale. *How to Win Friends and Influence People*. New York: Pharos Books, 1936. Print.

19   Carnegie, Dale. *How to Win Friends and Influence People*. New York: Pharos Books, 1936. Print.

20   Banks, Dylan. "57 Best Vulnerability Quotes." Marriage.com. June 10, 2025. Web. Accessed July 7, 2025. https://www.marriage. com/advice/relationship/vulnerability-quotes/.

21   Johnson, Michael Bassey. *Before You Doubt Yourself: Pep Talks and Other Crucial Discussions*. Independently published, 2021. Print.

22   "Elbert Hubbard Quotes." Goodreads. Web. Accessed May 17, 2025. https://www.goodreads.com/quotes/43331-the-greatest-mistake-you-can-make-in-life-is-to.

23   Middleton, Kelly, and Petitt, Elizabeth A. *Simply the Best: 29 Things Students Say the Best Teachers Do Around Relationships*. Bloomington, Indiana: AuthorHouse, 2010. Print.

24   Blanchard, Ken, and McBride, Margret. *The One Minute Apology: A Powerful Way to Make Things Better*. New York: HarperCollins, 2003. Print.

25   Customer Thermometer. "Unhappy Customers: Your Greatest Untapped Resource." Customer Thermometer. Web. Accessed May 17. 2025. https://www.customerthermometer.com/customer-satisfaction/unhappy-customer/.

26   Middleton, Kelly, and Petitt, Elizabeth A. *Simply the Best: 29 Things Students Say the Best Teachers Do Around Relationships*. Bloomington, Indiana: AuthorHouse, 2010. Print.

27   Blanchard, Ken, and McBride, Margret. *The One Minute Apology: A Powerful Way to Make Things Better*. New York: HarperCollins, 2003. Print.

28   Blanchard, Ken, and Bowles, Sheldon. *Raving Fans: A Revolutionary Approach to Customer Service*. New York: HarperCollins, 1993. Print.

29   "The Soup Nazi." *Seinfeld*. NBC. November 2, 1995. Television.

30   Middleton, Kelly, and Petitt, Elizabeth A. *Simply the Best: 29 Things Students Say the Best Teachers Do Around Relationships*. Bloomington, Indiana: AuthorHouse, 2010. Print.

31   Holley, Perry. "Making the Leap from Boss to Leader." Maxwell Leadership. August 23, 2023. Web. Accessed May 17, 2025. https://www.maxwellleadership.com/blog/leap-from-boss-to-leader/#:~:text=Leadership%20is%20Influence%2C%20Not%20Your,doesn%27t%20happen%20by%20accident.

32   Middleton, Kelly, and Petitt, Elizabeth A. *Simply the Best: 29 Things Students Say the Best Teachers Do Around Relationships*. Bloomington, Indiana: AuthorHouse, 2010. Print.

33   "Benjamin Disraeli Quotes." Quotefancy.com. Web. Accessed May 17, 2025. https://quotefancy.com/benjamin-disraeli-quotes.

34   Carlzon, Jan. *Moments of Truth: New Strategies for Today's Customer-Driven Economy*. New York: HarperCollins Publishers, 1989. Print.

35   Rogers, Rod. *Pastor Driven Stewardship: 10 Steps to Lead Your Church to Biblical Giving*. New York: Brown Books, 2006. Print.

36   "Desmond Tutu Quotes." Goodreads. Web. Accessed May 17, 2025. https://www.goodreads.com/quotes/7424-if-you-are-neutral-in-situations-of-injustice-you-have.

37   Rimm-Kaufmann, Sara, PhD., and Sandilos, Lia, PhD. "Improving Students' Relationships with Teachers to Provide Essential Supports for Learning." *American Psychological Association.* 2010. Web. Accessed May 17, 2025. https://www.apa.org/education-career/k12/relationships.

38   Roorda, D. L., Koomen, H. M. Y., Spilt, J. L., and Oort, F. J. "The Influence of Effective Teacher-Student Relationships on Students' Engagement and Achievement: A Meta-Analytic Approach." *Review of Educational Research* 81. 2011. Web. Accessed May 17, 2025. https://psycnet.apa.org/record/2011-26274-003.

39   Gregory, Anne, Cornell, Dewey, and Fan, Xitao. "The Relationship of School Structure and Support to Suspension Rates for Black and White High School Students." *American Educational Research Journal* 48. July 2011. Print.

40   "James Baldwin Quotes. Goodreads. Web. Accessed May 17, 2025. https://www.goodreads.com/quotes/18154-children-have-never-been-very-good-at-listening-to-their.

41   Hartford, Tim. "More or Less." *BBC Radio 4.* August 14, 2009. Archived from the original on October 1, 2020. Retrieved February 14, 2025.

42   Stephen R. Covey (@StephenRCovey). "'What you do has far greater impact than what you say.' - Stephen R. Covey #Action #Impact #Leadership #QOTD For more on The 7 Habits of Highly Effective People, visit here: https://resources.franklincovey.com/the-7-habits-of-highly-effective-people?fbclid=IwAR1Z_Kyl-IUuH1Yi91_2UzAOSNHviXkxcRpMk_SoDpwtAhXWHZQcLhGrAPI." January 13, 2021. Tweet. https://x.com/StephenRCovey/status/1349340643034861568?lang=en.

43   "Ralph Waldo Emerson Quotes." Goodreads. Web. Accessed May 17, 2025. https://www.goodreads.com/quotes/11079-what-you-do-speaks-so-loudly-that-i-cannot-hear#:~:text=Quote%20by%20Ralph%20Waldo%20Emerson,I%20cannot%20hear...%E2%80%9D.

44   Middleton, Kelly, and Petitt, Elizabeth A. *Simply the Best: 29 Things Students Say the Best Teachers Do Around Relationships.* Bloomington, Indiana: AuthorHouse, 2010. Print.

45   Schwantes, Marcel. "Warren Buffet Says You Can Ruin Your Life in 5 Minutes by Making 1 Critical Mistake." *Inc.* November 6, 2021. Web. Accessed May 17, 2025. https://www.inc.com/marcel-schwantes/warren-buffett-says-you-can-ruin-your-life-in-5-minutes-by-making-1-critical-mistake.html.

46   "Aristotle Quotes." Goodreads. Web. Accessed May 17, 2025. https://www.goodreads.com/quotes/44473-pleasure-in-the-job-puts-perfection-in-the-work.

47   "Dale Carnegie Quotes." Goodreads. Web. Accessed May 17, 2025. https://www.goodreads.com/quotes/33781-people-rarely-succeed-unless-they-have-fun-in-what-they.

48   Susskind, Alex M., Kacmar, K Michele, and Borchgrevink, Carl P. "Customer Service Providers' Attitudes Relating to Customer Service and Customer Satisfaction in the Customer-Server Exchange." *Journal of Applied Psychology.* February 2003. Print.

49   "Julius Erving Quotes." Quotefancy.com. Web. Accessed May 17, 2025. https://quotefancy.com/quote/1178516/Julius-Erving-Being-a-professional-is-doing-the-things-you-love-to-do-on-the-days-you-don.

50   Wargo, Eric. "How Many Seconds to a First Impression?" Association for Psychological Science. July 1, 2006. Web. Accessed May 17, 2025. https://www.psychologicalscience.org/observer/how-many-seconds-to-a-first-impression.

51   Klein, N., and O'Brien, E. "The Tipping Point of Moral Change: When Do Good and Bad Acts Make Good and Bad Actors?" *Social Cognition*, Volume 34(2), 2016. Print.

52   Craig, J. Dean, and Savage, Scott J. "Instructor Attire and Student Performance: Evidence from an Undergraduate Industrial Organization Experiment." *International Review of Economics Education* 17. July 22, 2014. Print.

53   Middleton, Kelly, and Petitt, Elizabeth A. *Simply the Best: 29 Things Students Say the Best Teachers Do Around Relationships.* Bloomington, Indiana: AuthorHouse, 2010. Print.

www.ingramcontent.com/pod-product-compliance
Lightning Source LLC
Chambersburg PA
CBHW051729020426
42333CB00014B/1230